The Art of Education
by Linda Dobson

"Dobson's basic premise is that 'the public school system in this country is based on a false definition of education. We are not educating our children at all. We are conditioning them.' Eleven chapters explore the 'wisdom' of the art of education, comparing public education practices with what we now know about natural education and with individual families' values and priorities. The next five chapters suggest the benefits of this art for individual parents, children, communities, and the larger society. Includes 'A Dozen Simple Starting Points' for parents who want to get more involved in their kids' education. Dobson's sources are a complicated blend, but she argues her case for family-centered education effectively."

—*American Library Association's Booklist, February, 1995*

From the Foreword by John Taylor Gatto:

Schools by their very nature interfere with necessary preconditions of an education, they interfere with development of a full human consciousness by preempting vast amounts of critical time, and too closely regulating critical experience at exactly the moments in early life when such interventions do most damage. If present government plans to extend schooling backward to the age of four, three, or even two, materialize I predict that the catastrophe of spirit we currently see in teenagers and young adults will grow worse.

Schooling trains you to be obedient to a script written by remote strangers who cannot care (except in the most abstract sense) where you sink or swim. Education demands you write the script of your own life, frequently with the help of people who love or care about you, sometimes alone.

Never make the mistake of thinking that a college degree gives you an education. Don't think you are educated because you have an official title. Those are traps for the well-schooled to fall into. A strong indication that education is happening occurs when you find yourself increasingly challenging the premises of experts or suspending judgment until you can check things out for yourself.

The Art of Education

Reclaiming Your Family Community and Self

by Linda Dobson

Holt GWS

The Art of Education
Reclaiming Your Family, Community, and Self
by Linda Dobson

Published by:

Holt Associates, Inc.
2269 Massachusetts Ave.
Cambridge, MA 02140

First printing April, 1995 Home Education Press
Second Printing 1997 Holt Associates
Printed in the United States of America by McNaughton & Gunn, Lithographers, Ann Arbor, Michigan.

ISBN 0-913677-14-0

For the freedom and happiness of all children, most especially my loving teachers—Adam, Erika and Chuck

No part of this book was supported by any institution, grant or fund. It was supported instead by a network of home educators, dedicated parents I am humbled to call friends and colleagues. To everyone who has provided me advice, an ear, a conversation, a letter, a phone call, a tape of a radio or TV program, a newspaper or magazine article—thank you for *connection*.

I am especially grateful to my family—Gary, Chuck, Erika and Adam—for help, but particularly for understanding me well enough to know when to assist, when to encourage, and when to stay out of the way. Thank you for *love*.

Special thanks to my dear friend, Lynn Waickman, for keeping up with reading as chapters unfolded, and for her family's learning life as constant inspiration. For information always useful and timely, appreciation to George H. Brown of the U.S. Department of Education Office of Educational Research and Improvement. I wish also to express my gratitude to Patrick Farenga for the time and critical eye he supplied in the final stage of the manuscript.

And to Mark and Helen Hegener, without whose vision and faith and dedication this work would not have seen the light of day, a heart full of gratitude for enhancing my life with yet another inspirational learning experience.

There is a creature that swims beneath the whale and feeds from the drippings of its benefactor.

After twenty-odd years of feeding from a very courageous author, I felt I knew this book as it was painstakingly written. But reading it in completion has indeed been a feast, like manna for a very hungry soul. Whatever education I have received, though, falls short compared to what the three calves growing alongside this mother who is teaching them to fish receive.

This is not a book about schooling. It is a wondrous book about life and learning; timely, exciting and, yes, revolutionary. It serves as one small spark lighting the candle that lights another and another, just as the Buddha spoke of consciousness, "the flame that goes from log to log."

With loving respect,

Gary Dobson

...The right kind of education is of the highest importance, not only for the young, but also for the older generation if they are willing to learn and are not too set in their ways. What we are in ourselves is much more important than the traditional question of what to teach the child, and if we love our children we will see to it that they have the right kind of educators.
                                                                    —Krishnamurti

CONTENTS

Part Two—Benefits of the Art

Appendixes

Index

Foreword

John Taylor Gatto

In a minute Mrs. Dobson is going to talk to you about education and about reclaiming yourself, but before she does her publisher has asked me, a long-time schoolteacher, to speak first. This is not so easy if you've spent your life in a job which requires a person to pretend he is a thinker of thoughts and an author of sequences which really originate in the antiseptic chambers of the Ford Foundation (or Carnegie or Rockefeller or The Twentieth Century Fund). By the time these thoughts and sequences have passed through The Businessman's Roundtable, The Federal Department of Education, The Educational Testing Service, The NEA/UFT, the Harcourt/Brace conglomerate, the State Department of Education, the city department of education, the district superintendent, the building principal, the subject supervisor, the local political club, and various pressure groups, it is dangerous for a teacher to be anything but a relay. Thinking for yourself is not a good way to get tenure.

The truth is teachers know a good deal about schooling but hardly anything about education. In my business you don't get paid for educating—and if you do it persistently nobody has any use for you. That's just the way things have to be. Can you imagine a school of fish where each fish thought for itself? It wouldn't be a school at all. Q.E.D.

Nevertheless, I've cast about for some use this schoolteacher can be to an enterprise about education and found a way—I'm going to reflect on what kind of ground educational seeds grow best in, what needs to happen before an education does.

1. The pre-conditions of an education came to seem to me—the longer I taught school—to be laid in an acceptance of the terms of mortality, that is they appear to be fashioned from an understanding of the obligations which have to be accepted to be fully human. This is a two-stage process, recognizing the obligations first then welcoming them so they are discharged lightly with a glad heart, not in some grudging, mean, or perfunctory way.

The longer I taught school the clearer it became to me that kids who wore their destinies easily—and I saw as many poor kids do that as rich ones—had a chance to be educated as well as schooled. While the others, their classmates, were only being trained like laboratory mice.

I worked in a school and did schooling for nearly 30 years, but I always felt like a fraud when well-meaning people called me an "educator;" to judge whether anyone deserves to be called an educator you need to ask children and even they don't know whether it's true or not until after they grow up. You have to see long-range results before you know.

Almost nobody I ever met has a good education. Our schools are a large part of why that's so, but not for any of the reasons newspapers offer—like bad teachers or bad kids. The reason is that schools by their very nature interfere with necessary preconditions of an education, they interfere with development of a full human consciousness by preempting vast amounts of critical time, and too closely regulating critical experience at exactly the moments in early life when such interventions do most damage. If present government plans to extend schooling backward to the age of four, three, or even two, materialize I predict that the catastrophe of spirit we currently see in teenagers and young adults will grow worse.

The first one hundred years of American schooling—up until about 1960—were less culpable in regard to comprehensive expert intervention in young lives because schooling prior to Sputnik had a strong part-time aspect to it. The hype had not set in yet and there were many different ways to grow up. How many of you are aware, for instance, that in 1959 — just a third of a century ago — 40% of all American engineers were self-taught? They didn't have college degrees.

In 1959 families, cultures, and traditions still held central in the lives of children and schooling was a modestly useful adjunct. The great American myths we retailed back in those days, even inside of schools, were of unschooled heroes like Benjamin Franklin, Thomas Jefferson, Andy Carnegie, Albert Einstein — men who made their way without the benefit of much schooling. But after 1960 all that changed, driven by massive and profitable interventions into children's lives by big government, big business, big private foundations, big universities, big psychology, and big utopian thinkers who itched for a programmatic society.

After 1960 there just wasn't any way to escape comprehensive schooling. Not for most of us.

2. I am very well schooled, but cannot claim to be well educated. I know I am not. What is missing is something I've been pursuing for years, and before I die I hope to recover what schooling kept me from learning: Who I really am. Who my father and mother really were. What our collective history signified.

For sloppy minds the expressions 'schooling' and 'education' are interchangeable, but most are aware that schooling is a trivial thing, sometimes useful but never essential, while education is a matter of life and death. An educated life is made up of self-determinations, of many free-will decisions courageously made and many penalties courageously accepted. Yet well-schooled people are determined externally by management, by experts.

When I say education is a matter of life and death I'm trying to indicate something precise: schooling trains you to be obedient to a script written by remote strangers who cannot care (except in the most abstract sense) where you sink or swim. Education demands you write the script of your own life, frequently with the help of people who love or care about you, sometimes alone.

Never make the mistake of thinking that a college degree gives you an education. Don't think you are educated because you have an official title. Those are traps for the well-schooled to fall into. A strong indication that education is happening occurs when you find yourself increasingly challenging the premises of experts or suspending judgment until you can check things out for yourself.

3. What I learned from watching kids for thirty years is that it's almost impossible to know your true self without knowing deeply your parents' true selves at the same time. No one can really live

easily without insight into our parents, and our grandparents, including insight into the culture they came from. Knowing your parents and grandparents takes time, however, and time is what schooling removes in great chunks. How a free people ever allowed the state to interfere to this degree in the minds of children I cannot imagine, but history tells us it happened gradually, by degrees, as lobsters are boiled to death.

Once children enter school the undermining and destruction of values they are taught at home is begun. The erosion of parental and cultural values is deliberate, and utterly subversive of the unity families need to be strong. In courses labeled drug education, sex education, and death education, children are taught that their parents' rights and wrongs are based on outmoded definitions, that parents' ideas are not reliable guides, that experts— always called "scientific" experts—are the best pathfinders to follow.

School people are fond of talking privately about bad parents, but they have no patience at all with the idea that schooling makes bad parents by removing their responsibility for their child's development, and by removing valuable time for parents and children to associate with each other.

Family is the only class of association impossible to duplicate, yet school slyly suggests that your family can be compared with all others, ranked on supposedly objective evaluation scales. After all, if sons and daughters can be ranked, why not the mothers and fathers? And if families can be so ranked, isn't it also possible to trade bad parents for good ones?

Quantifying family merit is another one of the big lies of schooling, like quantifying reading ability or tracking children according to their supposed future destinies. The actual truth is your family is necessary, irreplaceable, and quite incomparable with other families (except in irrelevant ways). Inside your family orbit you are automatically someone significant and special. Think of that for a moment: significance accorded because of who you are, and not because of what you do. This is an essential form of nourishment. It cannot be reliably supplied by strangers or even friends — only by the family over the long haul.

The reason some children survive twelve years of schooling lies mainly in parents who wittingly or unwittingly teach their sons and daughters to preserve an original temper deep inside, one indifferent to school people and school things.

The secret of my own success as a teacher was primarily that I set out to teach children how to be saboteurs of the system, how to get away with their sabotage, and what to do with the stolen time. I taught that an education must be at times a fairly lonely thing.

The classic error that good schools make is in programming an activity or an enrichment for every waking minute, they allow no private time or private space but subject their clientele to a constant barrage of attention, scrutiny, surveillance, ranking, group activity. It is monstrous.

And I tell you what is more, it is pornographic in a deep and profoundly literal sense of what pornography really is: spying on someone else's private business, demanding to know secret things you have no right to know.

Over the past two centuries we have deteriorated from a nation where people minded their own business to a nation where a huge percentage of the workforce — Christopher Lasch said 22% — is hired to spy on, to snoop, to tabulate, and to report on each other's behavior. We are not a factory full of machines to be tended. We are complex and mysterious spirits to be respected and approached with trepidation. My real value as a teacher began when I realized I had become a pornographer and decided to stop doing it. That was an important piece of my own education.

4. So an education as opposed to schooling is a fairly lonely thing unless you are lucky enough to be learning among your own family, culture, religion, neighbors.... and even then you need lots and lots of time alone, lots of absolute privacy.

With that in mind it's time to move on to the foundations of an education, which are nothing more or less than the foundations of self-knowledge and self-respect. From watching kids for 30 years I think those foundations consist of accepting four tremendous responsibilities. The earlier in life they are accepted the more certain the road to education is.

The first responsibility is a constant personal awareness of Good and Evil. If that continuum is too theological you might try Right and Wrong, as long as you keep in mind that the secular frame of meaning in the second pair must be based on law and ethical culture; nevertheless one or the other judgment is essential.

I've spent a considerable part of my adult life tracking the removal of this notion of good and evil from human affairs. In 1513 Machiavelli published his book, *The Prince*, which advised politicians how to live in a private universe beyond good and evil while keeping up a proper front. In the intervening half a millennium an immense coalition of special interests has arisen whose very bread and butter depends upon casting doubt on the existence of moral absolutes. This is the very heart of political science and it explains how our own government could deliberately expose its citizens to nuclear radiation hazards, why it released radioactive waste in the air over Hanford, why it conceived the Tuskeegee Syphilis Experiment where the black patients afflicted with that disease were deliberately left untreated, but were lied to about that and given worthless medication. And many other instances could be given.

Since Machiavelli every Western government, including our own, has felt itself above good and evil—and since Kant and Hegel every major government has felt aggressively justified in considering those moral terms quite relative. But pragmatic philosophers, behavioral and developmental psychologists, and the whole cantilevered empire of science, scientism, and scientistic social workers feel this way too.

The condition signals a great difference between family education and schools: One of the first things a family tries to teach its children is the difference between good and evil, right and wrong. One of the first things our schools do is destroy that distinction.

5. If Good and Evil are the first responsibility that has to be accepted, the second is the necessity for work. I stress 'necessity' because it is independent of personal wealth, cleverness, or genius. Education doesn't just happen, not even to the brilliant, but is only acquired by active involvement.

We live in a time that despises hard work. We live in a time where most of us avoid productive hard work. There are few jobs that ask for hard work, by which I mean close attention and hard effort over a long period of time, and so this need to find real work is thwarted by synthetic reality. By comparing the small product of personal labor (one hand-knit sweater vs. 100 machine-knit; a small garden plot vs. a thousand tons of vegetables grown with chemicals and machinery) we lose sight of the necessity of hard work, we are not able to grasp its lessons — which go far beyond lessons of production and consumption, lessons which go deep into the mind and character.

The third great responsibility that has to be accepted is development of self control, self mastery. Bureaucratic and military leaders regard that as a matter of following orders, but it is only that to a minor degree. Self control means you are able to follow your own orders. An unwanted byproduct of being constantly disciplined by others is either noticeable servility or regular outbreaks of rage and violence—a phenomenon long exploited by military minds.

In the last 200 or so years the most violent nation on earth has been, not accidentally, the nation which gave lockstep government compulsory schooling to the world. I never get tired of holding that fact up for inspection. A couple of German scholars and writers, Erich Remarque and Dietrich Bonhoeffer, had no trouble tracing German fury to the type of school discipline the government institution inculcates in children. Bonhoeffer said that W.W.II was the inevitable result of good schooling. Remarque attributed W.W.I to the lies of schoolmasters.

One reliable way self-control is learned is from situations which require natural discipline to negotiate successfully. Think of the timeless lessons taught by jumping a horse, or piloting a small boat. In both you may be crippled or killed if you don't know what you're doing. Is it any wonder that horses and boats have been the exercises of the ruling class cultures all over the world for thousands of years?

But the lessons of risk-taking needn't be class-based if we recognize them for what they are—ways to develop and test our self-discipline. Inexpensive analogies are everywhere for those who recognize what is at jeopardy when the obligation of self-discipline is ceded to strangers.

The fourth great responsibility which must be accepted as a precondition to taking control of life—which is surely the ultimate aim of an education—is the ability to accept loss, in particular losses which arise from your aging and inevitable death. Learning to accept these things with courage, wisdom, and even as a warrior might, with a glad heart.

In our time a childish utopian fantasy has gripped the official imagination, one that argues that death and aging should be regarded as deadly enemies to be avoided. I think that has crippled our collective ability to grow up. The immense amount of human energy and treasure devoted to that futile end keeps too many of us like angry, desperate children. Making death unnatural, lying to children about it, hiding it (supported by the growth of a titanic medical industry based on claims of chemical magic), the growth of a vast cosmetics industry and any number of other fantasy industries. Good for business but not good for the struggle to become fully human.

Earlier in this century we severed the young and their natural exuberance from our consciousness by locking them away in schools under the direction of strangers. Now we hide from death and aging as if by doing so they would go away. A world without young and old is a sterile, dead place. A world without past or future.

6. What I've tried to do here is describe a set of conditions which precede and accompany the acquisition of an education. I've said that based on my experience as a schoolteacher I don't think you can become educated without an intimate awareness of right and wrong, without a love for hard work, without a good degree of self control, and without an acknowledgment and acceptance of your personal mortality.

A masterful command of language and numbers is a petty, mechanical trick compared to these things. And when I say that I put stress on the adjective 'mechanical.' Having come to worship machines in the days of the French and Scottish Enlightenments we have come also to revere those accomplishments which can be quantified in statistical language, even though quantification in what makes us human is only a charlatan's trick.

There are a few formal schools in the United States set up to allow worthy goals to be pursued—a few but not many—and all of them private schools. Yet wherever I've spoken around the country to people courageous enough to keep their children home from school, courageous and wise enough to do that in the face of substantial opposition by the general culture, I've seen these pre-conditions for education being learned.

Now I'd like to close with a personal story. It took me about 25 years of watching children to figure out these principles and feel confident I was on to something. Then one day a few years ago I was talking about my discovery with a woman I met on a boat to Alaska. I was telling her how I had come to study silently my most successful students, students I was attracted to because they acted unknowingly as my own teachers. I'm talking about those kids who command respect from every stratum of the student population just for being the way they are; wherever kids like that exist everyone knows who they are.

Anyway, I was telling this lady I had found these four qualities well-developed in every single one of the truly successful children I'd seen, even though the age group I worked with was mostly only thirteen years old.

She listened to me patiently and when I was finished her face lit up and she said "Genesis!"

"What's Genesis?" I asked. I was puzzled.

And she repeated, "Genesis, the first book of the Old Testament. You just named the four burdens God put on Adam and Eve as the price of being human; they had to leave Eden and accept those penalties you were just talking about, and accept them gladly if they were ever to be redeemed. God said you had to climb over those four obstacles in order to regain Eden, but Science says No, there is no good and evil, you don't have to work—machines will do it, the right combination of psychological tricks will control behavior, self-discipline is unnecessary, old age can be fixed by medicine, plastic surgery, and prosthetic devices, and death can be postponed until science finds a cure for it."

As soon as I got back to my cabin I grabbed a Gideon Bible and read Genesis, perhaps for the first time. Sure enough, there it was. Set down thousands of years ago. Whether by human hands or divine you'll have to decide for yourself.

© 1995 John Taylor Gatto

Introduction

The Art of Education

You say you think today's education system is failing? You must be talking about declining academic test scores or violence or illiteracy, then. *That* way it is failing. But look a little closer. *That's* not the real business of education.

William Torrey Harris, our U.S. Commissioner of Education at the turn of the century, had a goal: "Substantial education, which, scientifically defined, is the subsumption of the individual." That is, Mr. Harris sought to place all individuals under a general principle, setting one standard for all.

Ever since, the business of public education has been to modify natural, individual expression into a socially acceptable sameness. On this score, today's schools are more successful than ever.

"But," you say, "I went through all of that and I'm OK." How OK any of us are is a judgment call. If you look to the proliferation of self-help books and classes, or the growth of psychology-related services in this country, I'd say most of us realize that something's wrong, even if we can't pinpoint exactly what it is. For our children's sake, we'd better figure it out soon. For our children's sake, we'd better take a look at what we call education.

Take a moment and ask yourself, "What does it mean to educate?" Jot down your thoughts on paper until you've covered all the bases. Does it mean learning basic skills to become a literate person? Being successful in the future? Learning a little about a lot of things? Or a lot about a few things? Wealth? Happiness? Possessions? All of the above?

In *The Britannica World Language Dictionary*, you find definitions that most likely correspond with your current way of thinking. "To develop or train the mind...," "To train for some special purpose," "To provide schooling for," etc. We're even told to look for synonyms under *teach*.

If we look closer, we see the verb *educate* came from the Latin *educatus*, from *educare*, meaning "to bring up." We're then referred to the word *educere*, described under "educe."

This says *educere* came from *ex*-out + *ducere*-lead. To lead out. Mmm, just the opposite of "to put in," or what we commonly consider the business of education. Could it be that from the very starting line we're going off track, pursuing a false definition that leads to a false goal and, therefore, false success? Maybe the public education system is succeeding so well with its covert business because we've been too lazy to investigate for ourselves the purpose, the meaning, the wisdom of true education. Well, no more. Let's explore.

When we unquestioningly accept the false definition of education, we need measurable, sustainable goals, just as a business does. (It might help if you think of a manufacturing business, or factory, here.) "Johnny must absorb the 3,589 facts as scheduled for third grade consumption within the next ten months." The process is predetermined, like making a Big Mac: one portion of math, followed by a plop of science, add a squirt of values training, throw on a handful of extracurricular activities. Johnny, parents and teacher enter a frantic race against time so that the 3,589th fact is in place just in time for the test that will measure whether or not he reached the finish line. To reach the finish line—with every element of the burger in its proper place—is what counts.

The business of public education must, at all times, be manageable. Coordinating the activities of hundreds or thousands of kids requires a place for everyone, and everyone in his place. Subjects must remain within the boundaries of their titles, neatly separated like the peas and mashed potatoes in a TV dinner tray. While this does not help a child gain understanding of any particular information's relationship to life, it does ease the strain on management. The peas can be counted, and the mashed potatoes will look the same today as they did five years ago. It may not taste good, it may lack nutrition, but by golly we're sure everybody's getting the same meal.

We sleepily accept that each young mind exists as an empty vessel that needs to be filled with an accumulation of facts and figures, and we accept that, once accomplished, this will lead our children to success. This term—success—the goal of our backwards educational practices, has itself been perverted. Schools spend lots of time teaching us a connection between success and job, money, materialism, and class status. There's even a lesson in relative success (your success depends on your classmates' failures) thrown in for free.

What's to stop us from broadening this definition of success? Can't the woman who discovers that turning cakes into works of art gives her the greatest joy have as her reward for work, not fame or fortune, but a sense of fulfillment? Can't we call her a success?

Or what about the family who finds life in the woods in a broken-down house harder but more rewarding and peaceful than the tension and crowds of the city? Can't we say these family members are succeeding in accomplishing that which is most important to them?

Of course we can. We need only change our perspective and reeducate ourselves to accept a broader definition of success, like *The Britannica World Language Dictionary* sets forth: "A favorable or prosperous course or termination of *anything attempted*." (Emphasis added.)

Changing perspective, particularly about success, is not easy. After hearing the old lessons for so many years, the same message continuously bombards our daily lives through TV, newspapers and magazines, bulk mail catalogs, friends, neighbors, and family. The old lessons run deep. But when held up to the light of scrutiny, they offer no truth. They offer, instead, conditioning that creates producers and consumers, the kind of conditioning needed to keep the economic machine of our country humming. And the machine has a voracious appetite.

If someone announced, "As of today, all U.S. schools are bankrupt. Anyone wishing to learn something should learn it at home," imagine the panic in households from Seattle to Miami! We, the people, would have to figure things out! But no matter how much this turned *your* life upside down, it wouldn't come close to the confusion that would rumble through the halls of every state capitol and in Washington, D.C. Schools would no longer hand out learning in controlled, measured doses—we, the people, might get *too* smart. They would no longer choose *what* we learn—we, the people, could learn about things we didn't like and work to change them. They would no longer tell us *where* we could learn—how in the world would they measure and compare us? They would no longer say *why* we learn what we learn—imagine if we studied about subjects and vocations that satisfy our own inner needs, instead of subjects far removed from our daily lives, and chosen by people who don't know us or anything about us. The education business would no longer prescribe *how* we learn—the book learned, card-carrying, professional teachers would have to make room for the community member who has practiced his skill, perhaps for decades, and shares his wisdom with anyone interested enough to find out about it. Schoolmen would no longer dictate, down to the very month and year, *when* someone should learn, say multiplication—it would be up to us to acquire skills when we found them necessary to our lives.

Are we capable of making these decisions? Of course. Do we believe we are capable of making these decisions? Sadly, I don't think the majority of us do. Our thirteen plus years in school taught us only too well that others should lead, that we should wait until we're told when, why and how it's important to know something. Schools and their peculiar brand of training are vital to our economy, not to us as thinking individuals. Knowledge and real learning—a truly educated populace—would send shock waves through everything politics controls.

The need to rebuild public education is obvious. But all the talk about school choice and longer days and teacher competency tests and Head Start for newborns (and yes, ever more money!) is like patching the bricks with Elmer's glue while we ignore the roof falling on our heads. All of these "patches," no matter how noble they sound, no matter how deeply we reach into our pockets, fail to reach the heart of the problem.

I want you to ponder, long and hard, a point I trust will shock you, anger you, horrify you, and/or awaken you enough to move beyond passively reading this book to actively carrying out your important role in reclaiming yourself, your children, and your community:

The public school system in this country is based on a false definition of education. Its path leads us to false goals. At the same time, the public school system does not follow the true

meaning of education. Therefore, *we are not educating our children at all. We are conditioning them.*

I hope this book leads you to connect a critical message about true education to our turbulent times and particular problems. Without connection, the message means nothing. With connection, you realize the key role only you can play in creating the solutions to the problems that daily destroy our children. Our lack of understanding is the only barrier between our children and a new foundation for a learning renaissance capable of vastly improving the quality of our personal, family, and community lives.

A dream, you say? Yes, it is. If we all change today, our grandchildren still won't enjoy the full fruit. But they'll see the tree growing. They'll catch the scent floating on the breeze, and they'll trust in the promise of a harvest for their grandchildren, the promise of education as art.

The cocker spaniel puppy licks ten year-old Jason's cheeks and nose before tumbling onto his back for a belly rub. "Let's call him Einstein, O.K., Dad? And, Dad, let's build him the best dog house ever!"

Dad and Jason work on the dog house plans at the kitchen table long past Jason's bedtime. The boy's rough sketches take shape as Dad explains how to draw to scale, how to use the roof as a shelter for the doorway, and how to save some money on materials with careful planning.

The weekend finally arrives, and Jason escorts Dad to the lumber yard. "Get a pound of six-penny nails," Dad tells the boy after they tie the plyboard and lumber onto the car. "And pick out a half-gallon of paint, too, please." Soon the materials and tools reach from one end of the family's garage to the other. Dad shows Jason how to measure and draw lines where the plyboard needs cutting. After a dozen mistakes, Jason turns the board over and tries again. This time he succeeds.

Over the roar of the table saw, Dad explains the necessary safety precautions with each step. They spend the rest of the afternoon hammering boards into place, checking for level and plumb, and making sure the tar paper and roof shingles will keep Einstein dry.

Jason applies the last stroke of red paint to the sign bearing

Einstein's name above the doorway as the sky slowly turns pink with the setting sun. The job is done.

Einstein will use his house many years. Jason will use his education for a lifetime.

The art of education is practiced like any other art—the product reflects the inner being of the artists. A Picasso is not a Van Gogh is not a Matisse, yet all possess their own beauty. Who is to judge which is more precious, more valuable, more worthy? The Smiths don't approach family centered learning like the Johnsons, and the Johnsons' practice doesn't look anything like the Dobsons. The masterpieces turn out differently, yet each radiates its own beauty.

When education is art, *the journey is the education.* That means today—this very moment—is just as important as any other. Suddenly every step holds significance, not just the one that puts you over the line. It is as if, having driven the same route to the same destination for many years, you notice for the first time the flowers in the park, the smell of bakery bread in the air, squeals of delight from a ball game in the distance. When every moment has meaning, your senses awaken, your mind opens, you're eager to proceed. Experiencing the journey allows the wanderer to reap a harvest of connection, of significance, of joy.

Education as art instead of business leads us gently to education's true meaning, its natural rhythm. But if we're not busy putting facts and figures into our children, what is it that we intend "to lead out?"

Ironically, it's those abilities that young children bring to life, delighting and amazing us with their natural, open expression. It's the abilities we adults realize we've lost, though we can't say exactly where or when. For the sake of brevity, I will list them: Curiosity, Imagination, Creativity, Inner Peace, Humor, Artistry, Self-Motivation, and Intuition. We are born with these abilities, witness the infant studying your face and smiling with recognition, or the toddler striving to perfect her walking technique, or the three year-old who shares a hug and a messy kiss at just the right time.

Were we to focus one-tenth of the time spent pursuing academics on nurturing what already exists, the remaining nine-tenths of our "school" time could be spent pursuing that which interests us, honing our unique skills. We would all be artists! Whether our life's work includes creating poetry, building ice cream cones, or investigating homicides, each accomplishment would emerge a masterpiece, a reflection of the best inside its creator.

Watch a stranger in the act of creation sometime. If she loves her work, it is evident in her eyes, her voice, her heart. She radiates from within, fueled by a constant repletion of energy.

If she does not love her work, the evidence comes from the same places. Instead of drawing energy from an abundant, internal source, the act drains energy—it is a chore, a burden, and she might as well be scrubbing toilets (no offense whatsoever to any who may enjoy this task of service—it, too, can be enjoyed). Her heart feels no difference.

When we nurture children, we "lead out" their natural abilities. We bring forth internal energy that only needs an escape hatch. When acts of learning draw the energy out (acts of learning being those acts motivated by curiosity, imagination, creativity, etc.), our lives improve in direct correlation. We feel healthier. We feel more content, foregoing the constant struggle for false success. We feel happier.

Many more of us could spend our lives "doing what we love," shedding light on the joy and rewards of pursuing personally meaningful interests. Happier parents raise happier children. Happier families live in more content communities. More content communities make for a healthier planet.

Any person, young or old, who consciously exercises just a few of these eight abilities can learn anything, anytime, anywhere. Even if you haven't seen traces of them in yourself in years, take heart. Like regular work-outs help build lazy muscles, exercising these characteristics will build them up again. It just takes time and attention. Remember, unless you taught yourself, *you* didn't get an education in school, either!

The art of education is practical and successful on small scales for now. Momentum to explore this alternative blossomed in the only place change of this magnitude is possible—within individual homes. Families practice the art in New York City apartments and Idaho farms, in suburban split-levels and rural log cabins, in African missions and in vans leisurely crisscrossing the U.S. Chances get better every day that it's practiced on your block, in

your school district, or somewhere within your town. It is practiced by people *just like you.*

There is nothing mystical or magical in practicing the art of education. It requires one step: You must wake up.

Granted, this is not an easy step, and even the dawn's initial
"mind stretch" may hurt a little or a lot, depending on how long
and hard you've been sleeping. But an open mind is essential.

An open mind needs first to be swept clean of negative impressions you may harbor about learning and school. These negatives
may include specifics, like a strong distaste for numbers and math.
Or they may be more general, like a fear or hatred of the authority
imposed by the teachers and principals who held the key to your
academic success or failure.

If your child approaching you with a science book makes your
hands sweat and your heart beat irregularly, you don't need to verbalize your fears. He'll know through your attitude that there
must be "something wrong" with the subject. What's worse, he'll
"learn" the general attitude, never quite understanding what that
"something wrong" is. Instead of learning something interesting
about science, he'll learn hate—or fear—through you.

The best remedy is to approach all learning adventures with
your children as if you are learning for the first time. You may be
surprised to discover that long division really isn't as bad as ol'
Mrs. Thompson made it out to be.

An open mind is not obsessed with doing "school" RIGHT
according to tradition. It's free to consider doing school WELL,
whatever that requires, to meet the needs and interests of the individual it serves. For instance, you discover your child is having
trouble getting started reading, and you hear about a new method
that utilizes music, or math, or even mud to get the job done. Your
neighbor may laugh, your mother-in-law may think you've lost
your marbles. But you know that, for your child, music's rhythm
motivates, math's logic inspires, or mud's mess mesmerizes.
Suddenly, you and your child are the best judges of the new
method's potential *for your family.*

As judge and decision maker you encounter a significant shift of
responsibility. You may view responsibility as a loathsome burden

or an exciting challenge but, in either case, placing it squarely on your shoulders is a direct sign of waking up.

After your mind stretch, take a big cup of Truth—straight up. Read, study, talk, think, meditate, pray. Truth will come. Like coffee, its innate ingredients awaken you. Unlike coffee, you can never get too much.

Shower yourself with good, simple things that honor your growing, inner abilities, and nurture these in your children—read together, laugh together, create together. If other activities you're currently involved in aren't helping stretch your abilities, they're probably hindering. Replace them. Complicated things need to give way before there is room for the simple. Only an empty cup can be filled.

I'm not offering you "10 Easy Steps" here, folks. We're talking W • O • R • K. You will examine a way of life you and everyone you know cling to, likely for fear of the unknown. The rewards are not concrete; you cannot hold them in your hand, you cannot count them like so many dollars or trophies. This is why the act of family centered education requires 1) courage and 2) trust.

And all of this for a mere whisper of a promise, a promise that life for you and your family can be happier, healthier, and more meaningful. It's a promise realized every day in a rapidly growing number of American households.

You *will* wake up, sooner or later. For as we, the people, sleep, an impersonal, ludicrously costly government assumes greater and greater control over our families and our communities. We are paying for our stupor with our children's lives, liberty and pursuit of happiness. This book is a wake-up call about taking responsibility for our children's education as a giant first step toward re-creating individuals awake and sensible enough to raise strong, capable families. Families that become the foundation of aware, safe, and responsive communities in a peace-filled world. Only we, the people, can do it.

And we, the people, must teach ourselves.

PART ONE

Wisdom of the Art

If fifty million people say a foolish thing, it is still a foolish thing.

—Anatole France

CHAPTER ONE

MEET YOUR MAKERS

When 2000 young men were asked to spell out their greatest concerns for the future, they expressed two major fears in equal weight—and absolute contradiction: fear of not having enough money, and fear of being locked in by the constant pursuit of money. To purchase freedom at the sacrifice of a comfortable life is virtually unthinkable. If only they could have their cake and eat it on Martha's Vineyard....

—Gail Sheehy in *Pathfinders*

Who are you?

If you answer this question with your name, your profession, your family relationship, your credentials, or any of the thousand labels worn in daily life, please pay attention. This chapter is written with love especially for you.

Before you can take conscious control of your destiny, before you can assume greater responsibility for your family, before you and your children can be assets to your community, you must know who you are. A difficult task, indeed, given years of training to look outside yourself for identity.

Who is the person, for example, called Sandra, working as a nursing supervisor, mother of Jennifer and John Jr., who graduated with honors and a Masters degree? Who is it who has this name, these children, this job? The answer for Sandra, as with all of us, exists inside. It is found, not by asking others or by identifying with the labels we wear, but by introspection.

There are dozens of methods to accomplish this, as well as thousands of books, videos, cassettes, and even technologically advanced machines with which to begin this process. Visit your local bookstore or library to get a feeling for what's available. Learn a little about the method that most readily captures your attention.

Once the journey of introspection begins, one of the first things many folks realize is that the image of a "self-made" man or woman is a myth. Frank Sinatra may *think* he did it "his way," but had he looked closely enough, he would have seen his personality, behavior patterns, likes and dislikes, dreams, and even his thinking were conditioned and shaped by the society and circumstances which surrounded him as he journeyed toward adulthood.

Outside influences blanket the true Self with layer upon layer of conditioning (or programming). Through the years, these layers pile up, rust into place, and crystallize a misplaced faith that who we truly are *is* this very rust pile. To find one's Self and answer the question "Who am I?" requires stripping away the layers of conditioning that hide our true nature.

It is impossible to recognize, let alone remove, these obstacles to our understanding of Self without at least a cursory understanding of what they are and where they came from. There are hundreds, if not thousands of these influences. Some are obvious—Mom, Dad, siblings and friends. Others are not so obvious—the quality of environmental stimulation and experiences changes the shape of your brain, your thoughts affect your environment, you tend to meet others' expectations of you, regardless of whether they are high or low. But for now, we're going to concentrate on the major social institutions that touch your life, for two reasons: 1) They are large and fraught with danger, and 2) their capacity for conditioning us is so well implanted in daily life no one escapes their influence. No matter where you live, or went to school, or how rich or poor you are, with regard to institutional conditioning, you're drifting in the same boat as every other American. Some of us got more, some less, but no one got missed.

So let's meet your makers, the institutions of American life that have, to date, shaped your thinking and directed the life you are leading.

Just Do It
(Or, Teaching You to Pay $100 for Sneakers with a Smile on Your Face)

Ah, money, up there on a pinnacle unreached by friendship, love, trust, honor, God or family. How much of your time revolves around greenbacks; waiting (to get the next batch), wishing (you could spend more), wondering (if there will ever be enough), and worrying (will it last until the end of the month)?

Make it. Spend it. Make more. Spend more. The merry-go-round makes you dizzy, even physically, psychologically, or emotionally sick. Yet you stay on, unaware that there are other rides to try, fearing what the future holds if you dare leap off.

Why do we do it? Is constant pursuit of the almighty buck *your* idea of the perfect life, or is somebody or something else pulling your strings, shaping your thinking and behavior?

First you must remember that to a certain degree the government, primarily through the power of taxation and public spending, can control quantities of available money. However, government officials have traditionally relied on the advice of investment bankers. In the product of over twenty years of research, *Tragedy and Hope: A History of the World in Our Time*, Carroll Quigley explains the results: "The history of the last century shows... that the advice given to governments by bankers... was consistently good for bankers, but was often disastrous for governments, businessmen, and the people generally."[1]

Furthermore, "The influence of financial capitalism and of the international bankers who created it was exercised both on business and on governments, but could have done neither if it had not been able to persuade both of these to accept two 'axioms' of its own ideology. Both of these were based on the assumption that politicians were too weak and too subject to temporary popular pressures to be trusted with control of the money system; accordingly, the sanctity of all values and the soundness of money must be protected in two ways: by basing the value of money on gold and by allowing bankers to control the supply of money. To do this it was necessary to conceal, or even to mislead, both governments and people about the nature of money and its methods of operation."[2]

In "Absolute Absolution," the author of *Dumbing Us Down: The Invisible Curriculum of Compulsory Schooling*, John Gatto, summarizes the omnipotent control of private bankers, stating that since 1914, we have allowed them "to determine the value of currency, whether business expands or contracts, and that these private individuals, who are mostly unknown to the public, have been given the magical power to create money or destroy it as they see fit."[3]

And you thought *you* made money! You simply earn enough to keep your place on the merry-go-round. But you must spend that earned money, too, for this is the fuel that keeps the merry-go-round operating. Private bankers and their buddy, big business, find getting you to do this is a snap—they advertise!

The purpose of advertising is universal: Create mass desire, then fill it. So marketing specialists study us, the consumers, more closely than scientists study lab rats. They measure our psychological processes, spending habits, TV viewing, hobby pursuits, and reading rituals so their messages take the most direct route to "targeted" markets: young or old, rich or poor, parent or childless, married, divorced, or owner of a three-legged dog in need of prosthesis.

My own informal study consists of a quick review of twenty

commercials on two major networks one evening (sorry, I couldn't take any more!). My notes reveal the following about us as trained consumers:

1) We can be led around by the nose with sex. Subconsciously stir our desire for sex, or to be sexy, and we'll buy your cars, beer, and toothpaste.

2) We desire to be just about anything we are not. Flash colorful, fast-moving pictures displaying people who have and do what we don't (and think we want), and we'll buy your hair coloring, diet shakes, and a pair of those $100 sneakers that let us make jump shots like Michael Jordan.

3) We like to think we can get something for nothing. Just tell us it's on sale, or you will throw something in for free, and we'll buy your hamburger, exercise program, and a knife that never needs sharpening.

4) We cherish things, worship sports players, compete with our neighbors, honor the ruthless, and use far too much medicine to relieve the symptoms of stress.
(Note: Big business, with lightning speed, is taking its scientific advertising methods and behavior shaping directly into your child's classroom. Be sure to read the chapter titled "As You Sow, So Shall You Reap.")

O.K., O.K., I want. I'll buy! But don't you dare make me wait for it!
Your programming in your "right" to immediate gratification was shaped by big business starting, perhaps, with credit and credit cards. If you are already working steadily enough, you can gain access to the privilege of spending money you haven't earned yet. What better way to insure that you'll stay on the merry-go-round for a few more spins? And if you buy enough on credit, you're entitled to a lifetime ticket!
It was nice, wasn't it, carrying a big screen TV out of the store, driving home, and enjoying it today instead of waiting two years until you gathered enough cash for it? ("I owe, I owe, so off to work I go.")

Of course, the price you pay for all the things you've been led to desire is determined by the value of your money which, of course, is determined by those nameless people previously mentioned who help create your desire in the first place! It's not your fault that big screen TV costs more than you could possibly pre-save for. It's not your fault all those commercials and ads (whose costs are simply added to the price of your TV) make it look like something you just can't live without. And it's not your fault that you feel your worth as a person just increased with your new purchase. (Where does *that* life-altering misconception come from?!)

There's also no need to wait until tomorrow for the money you *do* have; just use the automatic banking machine tonight. And while you're there, your computer silently adjusts your portfolio as the stock market fluctuates. Let it spend while the spending looks so good! My, but you use your conditioning well!

Immediate gratification conditioning even invades the more mundane life activities, like meals (and I use that term for "fast food" loosely), mail (fax it!), and shopping for pots and pans (yes, Ms. Jones, the XYZ Mail Order Co. delivers overnight).

You were not born to desire "things" and consume more rapidly than you can earn money. Consumers are created, programmed with scientific accuracy like Pavlov's dogs and sold something far more expensive than even the fanciest car you can imagine—the reality of a life spent spinning on the economic merry-go-round, chasing the fleeting pleasures of consumption while the money controllers push the buttons of your thinking and manufacture your next desire. Want more, earn more, spend more; the merry-go-round keeps on turning. Oh, and by the way, you now owe more taxes for the privilege of earning more money, which helps your next "maker," the government, grow even larger!

I Pledge Allegiance

Every society throughout time utilized some form of government to provide much needed services for the good of all. Problems occur historically not with the *form* of government per se, but when the individuals who comprise the government—be they kings, dictators, or presidents—lose sight of honesty, compassion, and civic responsibility under power's intoxicating glow.

Blind trust in an immense, life-or-death controlling institution is either an act of extreme faith or utter stupidity. One only need read a few newspaper or magazine articles to understand that medieval kings who feasted while the peasants died of disease and starvation had nothing on 20th century politicians. Cases in point:

Average number of members of Congress charged with a crime each decade between 1789 and 1970: 2. Average number charged with a crime each decade since: 24. (From *Harper's Index*, 11/93)

Checking two issues per week, an informal, two month study of my local, average twelve-page daily newspaper uncovered the following: NASA fraud, President Clinton's cheating heart, secret government human radiation experiments, Iran-Contra coverup investigator deemed former President Reagan impeachable, possible foul play regarding a White House attorney's suicide, questionable legal practices by First Lady, and a vocal campaign reform-advocating U.S. Senator who bought art and partied with his "leftover" $106,939 in campaign funds.

Imagine a newspaper reporting "George Washington should have been impeached for trading arms for hostages. Several militiamen also confirm having arranged trysts for George when Martha took leave of their Valley Forge residence."

Was my study a typical two months? Try it and see. Read with the eye of a naive colonist. Give it your complete attention or the reports are bound to slip by you, so familiar, tiring, and disheartening have they become.

The media is shouting at you. At the same time, there are many who work hard to ensure you do not wake up.

Today's government is not what our forefathers worked and died for. It has grown much larger, more powerful, and more intervening into the private affairs of its citizens than Thomas Jefferson could ever have imagined. That intervention has shaped your thinking and your life since you were born. Let's look briefly at its role in family life and education as one of your chief makers.

In *The Way We Never Were*, Stephanie Coontz explains that "child labor legislation and compulsory schooling aimed to root out 'precocious' behaviors among children, restrict them to home, and strengthen the adult male breadwinner role."[4] Family behavior, it seems, could be—and was—legislated. It's really quite simple: if you want people to behave a certain way, make it illegal for them not to.

The arm of government stretches beyond laws. It pulls the purse strings on assistance to families in need, too. In order to meet government requirements, families learned they had to behave (therefore, think) a certain way or be denied help during tough times. Some pooled economic resources or shared cooking facilities with others to cut costs (perfectly logical and emotionally satisfying ways to save money while getting back on their feet). These families found assistance held back until their behavior changed.

Before compulsory attendance laws forced children into schools, apprentice programs were a mainstay of education. Working adults offered learning opportunities to young men who swapped their sweat for on-the-job training, producing people like Benjamin Franklin. Franklin, who worked in his brother James' Boston print shop, learned his trade so well that he earned his way to Philadelphia, worked for another printer and, after a detour to England, set up his own shop at the tender age of 22. The free spirit in Franklin, incidentally, recognized that a borrower is a slave to the lender, so he quickly repaid the money borrowed to start his business.

Within one hundred years, though, the natural apprenticeship practice that helped so many young men had deteriorated into corrupt programs used, says historian Maxwell Bloomfield, as "a device for the recruitment and exploitation of young paupers." In Franklin's time, apprenticeships were considered a way to help families educate and socialize their children. But by the 1840's, government (and church) authorities gave themselves the power to relieve poor families of their children. Apprenticeships lost that loving feeling of community. They decayed into exploitation. Social services, the "helping hands" of government, were born.

American family life, especially for low-income families, has never recovered from the blow. Self-responsibility doesn't pay, our ancestors were conditioned to believe. Government slowly and systematically replaced the idea of man's home as castle with man's home as tendril of the institution of government.

(Note: The all-pervading government institution also encompasses military and law enforcement training and service, as well as string-pulling PACS and all brands of nationalism. But these aspects are worthy of books unto themselves! They have all worked as your makers. Take some time to examine their influence on the thoughts, ideas, and way of life you think are your own... that is, if you can find the time.

While government regulations may not *directly* overshadow your life, consider the fact that the U.S. Office of Management and Budget reported, "In the 1980's the private sector was spending over *5 billion hours* a year just to meet government paperwork demands. It is spending even more time...in the 1990's."[5] Federal regulations also cost Americans $395-510 billion in 1990. In spite of your government, find some time for thinking about reclaiming control of your own life. Good luck.)

In God We Trust

Strange how when I hear this phrase my mind doesn't turn to inner cosmic secrets or theological philosophies. The saying's appearance on government issue notes ($$$) seems, at first, an ironic attempt to bring God into an all-encompassing societal Trinity: Economy, Government, & God (probably incorporated to take advantage of the tax breaks). After all, Christ is credited with instructing us to "Render therefore unto Caesar the things which are Caesar's; and unto God the things that are God's."

Maybe there was too much separation inherent in this statement. Maybe it was easier to lull us back to sleep and into step if we, the people, never dwelled too long on the relative merits of the inner and outer world. Maybe if God could be assimilated into the outer world, we would never need to consider the inner world at all!

The government and economic institutions found what is really an ingenious solution—add God's name to that which belongs to Caesar! Weave the dominant Christian ethic (just enough so people can see it, now!) into every aspect of manmade law. Ta-da, the new Trinity was erected.

You're right, this is a rather simplistic view of how government lost God and found mass compliance. But we're here not to review the historic marriage of government and religion, but to understand how the shadow of this history falls over your life and shapes your thinking and behavior today.

The problem with religion as your maker is not religion itself. Religion, ideally practiced, is an intensely personal matter. A religious person's life—thoughts, work, play, self-regulation, acceptance of others, courage in the face of adversity and death—are an external expression of an active inner world nurtured and tended as a mother cares for an infant. A religious person's life radiates with a loving peace that has blossomed inside, touching everyone in its path as the flower's perfume simply floats on the spring breeze. Right action (what we today label as moral behavior) flows naturally from the inside out. Left unencumbered by society's institutions tugging his attention in a thousand different directions, a religious person is the most content, peaceful, happy soul you'll likely meet.

> Say nothing of my religion. It is known to God and myself alone. Its evidence before the world is to be sought in my life: if it has been honest and dutiful to society the religion which has regulated it cannot be a bad one.
> —Thomas Jefferson, *Works*, Vol. 7

The religious people in mankind's past—Gautama Siddhartha, Lao-tzu, Moses, Lord Krishna, Jesus Christ, Prophet Mohammed, and others—simply shared the fruit of their internal worlds, providing juicy bites for anyone so inclined. They never set out to "organize" religion. They certainly never worked toward massive institutions developed in their names. And even the institutions' developers would turn over in their graves if they could see what, in modern history, masquerades as religion.

More humanity has killed and been killed in the name of religion than for any other reason. Sunday church attendance passes for absolution of sins in the work and personal realms the other six days of the week. Values classes for the young replace moral living and understanding. Religiosity (excessive or affected piety) serves its bearer's ego no matter the cost to others. Religious leaders turn sexual abuse into a hobby. Behavior management via punishment and reward reaches new heights.

Rather than live the more virtuous, challenging and, at times,

difficult lifestyle of a true Christian, more and more institutionalized Christians fit the definition Ambrose Bierce included in his
Devil's Dictionary before he mysteriously disappeared in Mexico:
"One who believes that the New Testament is a divinely inspired
book admirably suited to the spiritual needs of his neighbor. One
who follows the teachings of Christ so far as they are not inconsis-
tent with a life of sin."

The decline in our standard for living a religious life has a pro-
found effect on you. With millions of us disconnected from the
personal nature of religion (private, internal understanding, after
all, cannot be monitored), the religion institution compels us to fill
our spiritual gap with adherence to its doctrine. When the spiritual well is empty, even a drop of tainted water brings hope.

And when you read next how school prepares us to accept the
institutions that surround us, you'll understand how we manage
never to notice that our individuality and very ability to think for
ourselves are choking on that poison.

Compelled to Attend

Can you think of a better way to insure that you will be "made"
according to the dictates of others than by forcing you, by law, to
appear at a government-funded, state-controlled institution where
you spend a predetermined number of years as part of a crowd
subject to constant scrutiny and evaluation? No, I am not talking
about prison. I refer to public school.

In August, 1991, John Howard, Counselor with the Rockford
Institute, told the University of Wisconsin Center faculty that their
university's catalog "acknowledges that education is a process in
which the student learns things the educational institution has
decided will be beneficial to the learner and to the society." The
catalog goes on to insure parents the university "will strive to fit
the student for civic responsibilities."

Dr. Bowen, President of Princeton University, called this type of
thinking "indoctrination in accepted ideas." The *American Heritage
Dictionary of the English Language* calls indoctrination "the teaching
to accept a system of thought uncritically." (As in do what you are
told; "they" know what is best for you; don't question authority.)

I call indoctrination the saddest abuse of human potential and the sorriest waste of human minds that could ever be imagined. I call it *shaping our thinking!*

And if colleges and universities ignore the true meaning of education and accept indoctrination as their function in society, what then is the purpose of all the years of schooling that lead up to college, starting at the tender age of five or, in many cases today, even younger?

"School," says Ivan Illich in *Deschooling Society*, "prepares for the alienating institutionalization of life by teaching the need to be taught."[6] This way you may spend the rest of your life seeking out and paying others for thinking you are capable of doing, if only you knew that to be true. But, sadly, not too many people making a living in the education business are ready to teach themselves out of jobs. Furthermore, "Once a man or woman has accepted the need for school, he or she is easy prey for other institutions."[7]

This is the essence of how school becomes what just may be your ultimate maker. Through the legal power to make you attend for a minimum of ten years, you are part of a captive audience *taught to uncritically accept* that 1) you need someone outside yourself to provide you an education, 2) your education need only ready you for confinement within yet other institutions, and 3) the value or truth of these notions should never be questioned.

This programming comes to you courtesy of the education institution representative closest to you—the teacher. This is not to accuse teachers of consciously conditioning you. They do their time in grade school, then move on to a college that not only espouses "indoctrination in accepted ideas," but there they train to perpetuate the same in future American classrooms! Through the *type* of training teachers receive, this becomes an unquestioned and, optimistically, unconscious part of the job.

In teachers' defense, statistics show one out of five leaves the profession within five years. The powers-that-be call it burn-out. I call it disillusionment. Living the life of an indoctrinator is not what they intended. Leading kids to the joy of learning, they discover, is absent from school agendas.

As for the teachers who stay, all that college time spent studying classroom management pays off as maintaining order and discipline become necessary priorities. Teacher-maintained discipline may keep the classrooms quiet and orderly, but it also delivers lots of thought-shaping. Consider just a few examples:

- Helping a friend is "cheating"
- An "institutional expert" should decide what and when you learn
- Doing irrelevant, mind-numbing chores is good for you
- You are not capable of evaluating your own work or worth
- You are in competition with your classmates for your teacher's limited time and attention
- Answer, don't ask questions
- Time is too short to spend it listening to your ideas

Fortunately there's usually only one teacher promoting these lessons in each classroom. But an equally insidious and important force shows up in greater numbers—your peers.

What is the criteria for choosing these very important influences on your life?   Your peers happened to turn five or six about the same time you did, and their parents happened to move into the same neighborhood as yours chose. You wound up together in the same neighborhood school "because it was there."

Of course you didn't realize it at the time, but these fellow "little people" shared their sometimes less-than-correct knowledge (Moms swallow watermelon seeds then have babies), bigotries (all *fill in a nationality or skin color* stink), likes (I want green; Billy likes green), dislikes (Susan says spinach is awful; I don't want any), family dysfunctions (every time he gets mad he punches me!), and many more, bombarding your developing mind daily. The knowledge available within the experience of a fellow five year-old, however, does little to advance your academic career and less to guide you toward maturity. The old cliche about the blind leading the blind was written, I suspect, by an elementary school teacher eavesdropping on student conversations on the playground.

It stands to reason that if a group of people is arranged, as in public school, to be as homogeneous, or similar, as possible from the very start, is subjected to intense observation and criticism of minute details of behavior, and is then conditioned/programmed/taught the same things at the same time (without individual interests, thought, or ability entering the picture), the results are predictable. We wind up with "graduates" who "will no longer be surprised, for good or ill, by other people, because they have been taught what to expect from every other person who has been taught as they were." [8]

John Taylor Gatto, retired thirty-year veteran of New York City public schools and recipient of the New York State Teacher of the Year award, takes the horror of this "robot" effect one step further. He proposes a well-researched thesis revealing how the progressive education movement, working to cleanse the public schools of a colonial, "angry God" Christian curriculum, succeeded in their goal. Unfortunately when this "angry God" disappeared, so did "the idea of God along with him." [9]

If this is true it explains how public school programming has managed to create a society void of internal moral motivation and filled with hate, violence, and distrust. These are side effects of public school conditioning creating a society devoted to the economy, providing "busy work" for the masses who, in our sleep, are *powerless* to protect ourselves from the moral bankruptcy of the nation's political, economic, church, and education "leaders."

Armed with skilled—and due to additional programming, comatose—social workers and institutionally trained teachers, backed by law and armies of enforcers in every town and village (all funded with huge sums of taxpayers' money and, incidentally, trained to observe and report on fellow citizens' thoughts and actions), schools offer the perfect place for all your makers to converge, full force, on the young innocents gathered within the confines of the institution. You might call school the ultimate "institutional melting pot," the great equalizer. Under their methods, the needs and interests of individuals don't need to be met—they can be ignored!

Historians have collected materials containing Thomas Jefferson's view of American education ideals. In 1818, Jefferson set forth six objects of primary education which, with his knowledge of the people of his time, he calculated would require three years of schooling to achieve:

• To give every citizen the information he needs for the transaction of his own business;
• To enable him to calculate for himself, and to express and preserve his ideas, his contracts and accounts, in writing;
• To improve, by reading, his morals and faculties;

• To understand his duties to his neighbors and country, and to discharge with competence the functions confided to him by either;

• To know his rights; to exercise with order and justice those he retains; to choose with discretion the fiduciary of those he delegates; and to notice their conduct with diligence, with candor, and judgement;

• And in general, to observe with intelligence and faithfulness all the social relations under which he shall be placed."

While it is true Jefferson saw those three years of education as the state's duty, according to Merrill D. Peterson, author of the Bancroft Prize winning *The Jefferson Image in the American Mind*, Jefferson specified education should be "secular and practical, a matter of local initiative and responsibility, and *as free as possible of any coercive discipline.*"[Emphasis added.] [10]

"It is better," Jefferson understood, "to tolerate the rare instance of a parent refusing to let his child be educated than to shock the common feelings and ideas by forcible asportation and education of the infant against the will of the father."[11]

Thirteen-year long, legally enforced compulsory attendance was not part of the plan. Public school today is a far cry from the ideal public education Thomas Jefferson envisioned as his country's great equalizer. By the time we're all done boiling in the great institutional melting pot, everyone emerges the same. And void of awareness of the idea of God (or awareness of our spiritual aspect), that means cowardly. Ineffective. Valueless. Lazy. Amoral.

But equally so.

As a young girl teachers loved her. When no one else knew the answer, proudly she held her hand high. Homework arrived on the teacher's desk neat and complete. Like a bird above the clouds she flew straight and strong through all her school years until she graduated high school with straight A's.

She thought jobs would be easy to snag, and she was right, for she had learned to play the game by the schools' rules which were, in reality, society's rules. All grown up, she was intelligent (her I.Q. said so!) and free (out on her own at last!). Or was she?

"Now I can live!" she thought. She had money, a nice apartment, and plenty of friends. But emptiness surrounded her day and night.

"I became who 'they' wanted me to be. Now, who am I?" I wondered.

As you sort through the cobwebs of your mind and Self, your vision clears and more of the "whole picture" comes into view. You will discover how society's institutions cleverly encourage conformity and complacency by conditioning you in the fine art of submission to faceless, nameless superiors and self-serving rules, complete with subsequent punishment for transgressors and ample rewards for the obedient.

Yes, these institutions are untouchable, entrenched with time and supported by money, laws, and each other. But there is one thing you are in a position to change, and that's *you*. Rising to this challenge can have some miraculous benefits for your family and community. Read on. There *is* something you can do.

CHAPTER TWO

IS THAT ALL THERE IS?

At the end of your life you will never regret not having passed one more test, not winning one more verdict or not closing one more deal. You will regret time not spent with a husband, a friend, a child or a parent.

—Barbara Bush, 1990, from a speech delivered at
Wellesley College, Wellesley, Massachusetts

A neighbor called one morning, frantic because her day required a couple of long distance trips to get several family members to necessary doctor appointments. No matter how she figured her time and travel, getting her son to kindergarten just didn't fit into the puzzle that was becoming the day ahead. Even with my help, his attendance at school just wasn't falling into place.

I finally said, "It sounds like it will be easier on everyone if you just take him with you."

"Can I do that?"

"Excuse me?"

"Well," she clamored, "I never thought about him missing school."

"Whose kid is he, anyway?" I asked. "As his mother, don't you think you have some say in what's best for your family today?"

"I never thought about it like that before."

It is a good bet that if you have school-aged children, your family's daily routine and habits are *strongly* influenced by school's presence in your life. Perhaps, like my neighbor, you have never thought much about this phenomenon, either, so here are a few questions to get your mind in gear.

Have you ever read an ad for an enlightening seminar on astronomy and wished your son could go, if only he wasn't in school? Has the opportunity to take daytime aikido classes arisen, but you don't want to "ask" the school if your daughter can leave for an hour or two once a week? How about a one-night appearance of a symphony in a city several hours away, but, no, the kids have to get up for school the next day? Grandma is very sick in another part of the country, but you don't go care for her because the school frowns upon extended absences? You've been offered a job that could provide much more personal satisfaction, but changing schools would be too traumatic for the children?

Have you thought of other circumstances that apply to your own family yet? Most families bump into these or similar situations at one time or another. Each one represents missed opportunity, a lost chance for pursuing a personal interest, experiencing unusual or grand occasions that could spark new interests, or fleeting moments that, in cases regarding Grandma, may never be reclaimed and, more often than not, lead to regret that injures us for a lifetime.

In trying to cut down on truancy, some schools enforce a program that separates "excuses" into what may be termed legal or illegal. This boils down to school administrators deciding ahead of time the reasons why a family could allow its children to miss school. Since this need be done on a school-wide basis, individual family circumstances rarely enter the picture, let alone the family's belief of what is and what is not valuable to its children. This attitude about school attendance leads us, collectively, to accept that school—its schedule, its requirements, its queer notion of education—should unquestioningly rate the center of your family's universe.

This perspective of forcing children into classrooms, remember, arises as part of a misguided attempt at education to begin with. Now here's a deeper aspect to consider: When it comes to being prepared to live a good, healthy life, *is that all there is?*

No one would argue that intellectual growth and stimulation are not important to us as human beings. Yet through the attitudes and behavior cultivated in us by our makers (the ones we met in the previous chapter), we, as parents, let this objective run our lives as if it is the *only* significant aspect of our children. It's fundamental to remember this is the same education it was so important for today's adults to get. Now the same businesses that helped create the self-serving curriculum you studied have found it in *their* best interest to get "lean and mean," and to use technology to "downsize." Even those who learned their lessons well find themselves in long unemployment lines, shocked and numbed by the reality that what they considered a successful life yesterday is today as disposable as a used Pampers diaper.

Standing alone, mere intellectual development falls far short of providing your child with an education worth having, let alone a life worth celebrating. I think at some very deep level kids intuit this. I don't think they intellectually grasp what's going on, nor could they necessarily put their feelings into words, for words exist in the realm of the intellect. Consider Benjamin Barber's words written in late 1993: "Dropping out is the national pastime, if by dropping out we mean giving up the precious things of the mind and spirit in which America shows so little interest and for which it offers so little payback."[1]

Folks, I warned you this is a wake-up call, and truth hits as hard as any cold, wet rag across the face. The truth is America in the above sentence is our society as it exists today. Not America as Thomas Jefferson imagined it would be, nor Lincoln, nor the Roosevelts. Even Kennedy did not speak of today's America, for the full impact of the Technological and Information Ages was still only in his imagination.

Today technology and information and their immense influence on society are reality, continually changing the way we live. And if you'll examine those changes closely enough, for your children's sake, I trust you'll find that they have taken us away from the meaningful, the "precious things of mind and spirit," in a constant pursuit of the meaningless, all for the sake of the economy and the government, all under the guise of perpetuating democracy.

Were we even attempting to live up to our democratic ideals, we would not need education reform. The problem starts with our actions, everywhere in society and particularly in the classroom, for our actions do not demonstrate the example only we can set. Our forefathers' words are empty, existing only in classroom text books that do not reflect the society kids see before them today.

We teach our children that money is a top priority by our example and because their schooling—which takes an inordinate amount of their time and controls their families' schedules and lives—focuses on their place on the economic ladder of tomorrow.

Folks, if parents don't show their kids what's important in life, nobody else will. Your kids miss out on umpteen opportunities to join in real life learning, gracefully practicing the art of education, because they are compelled to attend school. A school, as Barber writes, where at least in the elementary grades, "an able student can be absent from school for an entire week and, quite literally, catch up with all he has missed in a single morning." [2] Benjamin Barber writes: "Yet for all the astonishing statistics, more astonishing still is that no one seems to be listening."[3]

If life is more than feeble attempts at intellectual stimulation and preparation for jobs, and you are beginning to see how compulsory attendance requirements undermine the natural flow of learning within the context of family life, it's time to look at what is happening to children in school at yet a deeper level.

The Gift of Time

Much attention has been paid by researchers and the media to the academic success of family centered learners. However, for home educators, academic success is not all there is. They realize that "men cannot remain content with what is given them by their culture if they are to be fully human."[4] So what do they provide their children that schools cannot?

Self-knowledge: "...the basis for serious, humane learning."[5] An understanding of who it is doing the learning.

Interestingly, families don't necessarily start out with this as a goal, nor is there a specific part in their curriculum or time of day when they study Self-Knowledge 101. Rather, this knowledge is a side effect of the family way of learning. It is an important by-product received because the family possesses a valuable commodity anyone trapped by a school schedule envies—TIME.

Young children use this time pursuing the path to self-knowledge through play. Play is your child's spontaneous, joy-filled embrace of life. In play, no walls divide the players from each other or pull the outer child away from the true Self.

It is here, in the Kingdom of Infinite Possibility, that your child physically, mentally, and spiritually strengthens her bond with true knowledge. The value of play lies not in relieving boredom or even in its ability to teach. Play is a child's most important work, providing the opportunity to express all that exists inside. It is at once a way to express—and define—Self. Children learning at home tend naturally to utilize their precious gift of time in play, thus gathering the blocks that create a solid foundation for the learning process.

Spend five minutes following your young child while she is in active mode. She will find this amusing at first; join in her laughter. She will try to tailor her activity to please you; allow her to lead. She will share with an openness and honesty with which you are unfamiliar; be humble in her presence.

Do not think about the electric bill; it will still be there when

*you are done. Do not worry about dinner; no one will starve if it
is five minutes late.*

*She has much to teach you. You have much to learn. Never
will you find a more loving, forgiving, unconditionally accepting
guide. She will not fail you, for it is not her intention to find
your faults. Rejoice in this sharing. Her heart and yours are one.*

The understanding that we all co-exist on one tiny planet with a
delicate ecosystem is sweeping the globe. But just as we harm the
planet by tinkering with nature's plan, we harm children when we
tinker with the marvelously ordered, delicate blend of mind, body,
and spirit that they are.

A child with time for experimentation and experience grows in
Self-knowledge. All aspects of her being—physical, mental, and
spiritual—receive attention, watered like a budding rose in a
spring rain. It doesn't rain in specific areas for allotted amounts of
time, training the child that each area stands alone. Every aspect
is part of the whole exquisite landscape, a picture made more
beautiful because of natural balance.

Those children who intuit their education isn't worth a hill of
beans feel the absence of balance in their lives. Adding a class for
ethnic studies onto the daily schedule doesn't bring the spiritual
aspect of a child into balance with the intellect. Likewise, a forty-
five minute weekly discussion of self-esteem and lists of the "10
Things I Like Most About Myself" don't lead a child to emotional
stability. School practices still leave spirituality, emotions, and
physical learning hanging out on a limb far removed from other
"subjects" of learning. They become only more subjects tacked on
to a long list of irrelevant, disconnected, "informatory knowledge."

"Present systems of education in various countries of the world
only give the students informatory knowledge," says Maharishi
Mahesh Yogi, founder of the Maharishi International University in
Iowa. "There is nothing precise in the field of education today
which will really develop the inner values of mind, body, and spirit. Therefore, whatever education is received by the people is just
on the surface level of information."[6]

Emptiness exists where education should fulfill our children.
The inability of informatory knowledge to satisfy, to quench the
thirst for knowledge every child possesses is sad enough. But the

continued practice of school-style intellectual development that strips children of their natural desire to learn, and robs them of any sense of integration, or connectedness, is a sin.

In order to gain a better understanding of the fundamental differences between an education that leaves your child wondering, consciously or subconsciously, "Is that all there is?" and education that brings balance and purpose to your child's life, you need to get a close-up view of both. Let's take a look at the Education Pyramid.

CHAPTER THREE

THE EDUCATION PYRAMID

Let not thy learning exceed thy deeds. Mere knowledge is
not the goal, but action.

—Talmudic Axiom

A little explanation is in order before we continue our deeper look at schooling and the art of education. A lot of us are tired and disgusted with our generation's focus on self. We have seen the ancient message of self-knowledge, passed down over millennium through every major religion on earth, twisted and turned until its wisdom serves a generation nursed on materialism, teethed on immediate gratification, and educated in a social environment of hostile corporate takeovers, get-rich-quick schemes, and criminal politicians.

This atmosphere has produced narcissism, not self-knowledge. The former focuses on gain, a "What's in it for me?" mindset, a belief that the singular "I" is the center of the universe. The latter, however, is a journey into one's inner world and spirituality, leading you ever closer to compassion and the knowledge that "I" is an illusory separation from a singular universe.

So please, as you read, do not confuse self-knowledge with narcissism, self-centeredness, or selfishness. Think of Self-knowledge as awareness, as a life of quality. The others represent dark sleep, a life of quantity.

> The aim of education is the acquisition of the art of the utilization of knowledge. A merely well-informed man is the most useless bore on God's earth.
> —Alfred North Whitehead

Unfortunately we have been led to believe that it is through the child's mind that he will reach awareness. But just as rocks are collected and piled one atop the other until, as a group, they form a dam capable of restricting the natural flow of a raging river, thoughts (products of mind) hinder the rhythm of consciousness. They create an impasse, separating the force of energy and intelligence from the pool of "outer" life. In reality the mind impedes awareness. To relate this understanding to learning and the true meaning of education, we must examine the nature of the mind.

In our normal waking state all information the mind admits is perceived through the filter of our senses. From the first day of life, this information is understood only in relation to what has passed before. It remains unchanged, in the same order and the same relation with previous impressions, not as they necessarily were, but as they were perceived.[1]

Since the mind relies upon sensory data, it continually desires stimulation and constantly requires experience. In this attempt to satisfy itself, it seeks the most pleasurable experience available. So attention constantly drifts: our focus transfers to pleasant music while reading the newspaper, an attractive member of the opposite sex passes down the street and interrupts our thoughts, we watch the gym class exercising outside the window during math class. But the mind will never reach contentment in the ever-changing relative field because new experience is continually created and, therefore, desired.

The object of experience fills the mind like a motion picture fills the screen at a theater. The pure whiteness of the screen (consciousness) is veiled in the changing motion of color (experience) produced by the camera (senses).

But for education to occur, one must know what remains as a *result* of the experience, *not the experience itself*. Learning, therefore, is the product of the union of the knower and the known. This union can only occur when pure consciousness remains unbound by the impact of the experience on the mind. When mind exists on the stable foundation of Self-consciousness, it is in a state of contentment and capable of serving in its true capacity—the link between spirituality and material life, a bond between the relative and absolute states of being.

When a person whose consciousness is lost in experience attempts to learn, the lack of foundation becomes apparent. This is why a child who managed to receive an A on a test can no longer remember the facts two months later. The information was merely an experience the mind perceived as opposed to a true fusion of the knower and the knowledge, the witness and the witnessed.

Imagine a three-year-old child's first experience with a car's engine as an example of a mind relying solely on sensory input. He sees a wonderful conglomeration of nuts, bolts and wires; something to touch and play with. When the conscious mind is brought into play, we have an auto mechanic who views a marvelously ordered, structured work of art. Both child and mechanic observe the same machinery but they acquire totally different perceptions because the mechanic's understanding transcends the experience of the engine.

There are many psychotechnologies available today through which you may expand your awareness. Meditation, from the Sanskrit word meaning "doing the wisdom," is a good, inexpensive, simple, easy place to start with your children as a family. (Check out the reference section for some good starting materials.)

Please don't let words like psychotechnologies and meditation scare you into erecting walls your rational mind won't scale. Your life has room for any form of meditation when you throw away the image of incense-burning, robed monks prostrate before an altar. "Doing the wisdom" simply means allowing yourself the time and space for introspection. In fact, it's probably something you already routinely do, under labels like prayer or contemplation or, perhaps, without even labeling it at all.

> Yes, we meditated—not always by sitting down cross-legged, trying to direct our erring thoughts toward higher realms. We might start the day with a recognition of our relationship with the whole, opening ourselves to an acknowledgement of the creative forces in the universe, keeping wide the channels of our being so that benign forces could stream through. We breathed especially deep of life at those times, and tried to continue this sense of dedication throughout the day. Was this meditation? For us it was.
> —Helen Nearing in *Loving and Leaving the Good Life*

For one of my friends, meditative states sneak up during quiet canoe rides. Another friend finds that once she travels deep enough into the woods, the rhythmic crunch-crunch of snowshoes helps empty her mind of life's trivia. Long walks or drives, quiet moments alone at home or in the office, horseback riding, gardening, sewing, hanging laundry, doing dishes—all provide opportunity to quiet the "monkey mind" and uncover the wisdom within. My point is that you don't have to wait for these moments; you can consciously create them, allowing yourself additional opportunities to reach a place where daily distractions momentarily disappear and you find the peace and knowledge Christ called "the Kingdom of Heaven" within.

It is unfortunate that so many people steeped in institutionalized religions confuse the universality of these practices' benefits

Education Pyramid

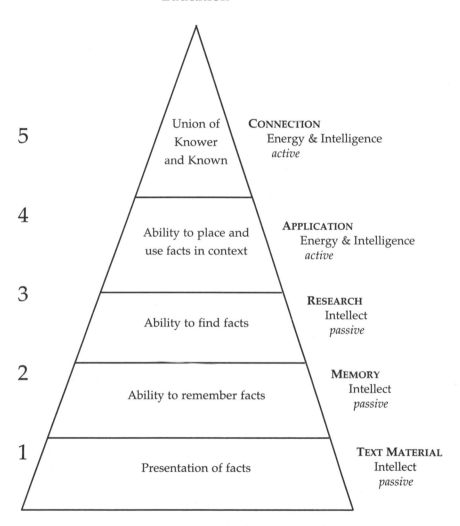

with an experience of "humanism," "witchcraft," "New Age," specific meditation methods, etc., and don't understand the difference between catholic spirituality and organized religion. Because of these misconceptions, schools fear meditation's inclusion in children's daily lives because of separation of church and state. The benefits, though, are real. And increased consciousness and awareness are vital to your child's educational experience, no matter where it occurs.

We have educated so exclusively to specialized training for life's "work" that we confuse intellect with intelligence. Intellect is thought void of emotion; the sharp, calculated, trained response. If we apply the cosmic, eternal definition to intelligence, we cannot separate creative intelligence from love. True intelligence involves an integration of feeling and reason, rendering the ability to understand life and internalize right values.

True learning requires thought. Thought has energy sending it and creative intelligence directing it. The art of education requires both energy and intelligence.

Now on to the Pyramid. The bottom of our Education Pyramid shows the simplest level of learning. Facts, or information, are presented to the learner as second-hand knowledge from text books. It engages only intellect, and is the most passive way to supposed education. (And isn't it really programming?) Information is thrown at the learner and his involvement in the process is minimal.

The second level involves memory and an ability to remember the second-hand facts, but this type of learning also stagnates at the intellect and is something "done" to the learner. As a fifth grade teacher in Oregon laments, "some [kids] seem to have forgotten how to learn without visual stimulation and affirmation of what they hear. Concentration and memory are just not as important to them."[2] As poor a substitute for learning as Level 2 is, this teacher's description seems to indicate that too many public school students are stuck at or below this level today.

Level three, an ability to find one's own facts about a given subject (research), engages a higher level of intellect. This level requires a bit more effort on the learner's part than the previous two. Instead of having the second-hand facts presented on a silver platter, the learner needs to first track down information on a given topic, separate the wheat from the chaff by deciding which bits of facts are relevant to his focus, then place all those facts in an orderly manner so they may be communicated to another.

You may remember from your own school experience that this activity appears to represent the epitome of accomplishment in institutional learning. A research paper, or report, or speech supposedly relays to the teacher your grasp of the subject. This paper oftentimes counts for a large portion of your final grade. And after you sweat over its preparation, after the teacher marks it up with a red pen (making it look like a whitewashed wall covered with graffiti), after the final judgment—the grade—appears at the top, you file your research paper away. (Maybe in the circular file?) In spite of the time contributed to this activity, the ability to find facts is still just a passive experience.

> But if one looks at what actually goes on in the classroom—the kinds of texts students read and the kind of homework they are assigned, as well as the nature of the classroom discussion and the kinds of tests teachers give —he will discover that the great bulk of students' time is still devoted to detail, most of it trivial, much of it factually incorrect, and almost all of it unrelated to any concept, structure, cognitive strategy, or indeed anything other than the lesson plan. It is rare to find anyone—teacher, principal, supervisor, or superintendent—who has asked why he is teaching what he is teaching.
>
> —Chas. E. Silberman in *Crisis in The Classroom*

Levels 1, 2, and 3, then, are typical school approaches to education. Regardless of their difficulty level, they all fall under the broader category of book learning. As you can see from the pyramid, these approaches require use of intellect, trained response. At these three levels, the learner gets "just the facts." The facts are perceived by the mind and can only be connected to previous understanding. In other words, if enough information isn't already "on file," additional bits and bytes of information (the type that come from writing research papers) sit there like lumps of coal. They cannot serve the learner in any useful capacity because they do not get connected; they do not "increase" knowledge.

And just to add to the confusion, there is no guarantee that the impressions received from these activities enter the mind free of mistakes, misunderstandings, or misconceptions. How the impressions are *received* depends on the condition of the individual's filter, or senses. The way information is *perceived* ain't necessarily the way it is!

Take a deep breath—you're three-fifths done! And now we reach the exciting part. You'll see how—with the freedom to direct your child's education yourself—you can guide him to the higher levels of the pyramid which rise above rote, book learning into the art of education.

Level 4 is called Application because here knowledge that the learner possesses from whatever source goes to work. Your child, vigorously engaged in activity, *uses* the facts in context.

Take ten year-old Billy Bob Raynor of Virginia, for example. One night he watched a news story about hungry, homeless children living in Brazil's sewers. Through family centered education, he has learned to use intelligence instead of intellect. The plight of the children touches his heart, thereby capturing his attention. Because his family has "the gift of time," here's what unfolds :

> *Off to theater rehearsals and performances that he enjoys. The Brazilian children are never far from his thoughts. At last, he earns a paycheck as a Munchkin in "Wizard of Oz."*
>
> *"The hardest thing," Billy realizes, "is trying to find out how to do it, who to send the money to."*
>
> *He searches until he finds WorldVision, and donates his paycheck. "As soon as I am old enough I want to go to South America, find these children, and bring them home with me. I would feed them and provide schooling for them."*
>
> *Following his interest, Billy Bob Raynor has learned how to track down information and write letters, skills he'll keep. He has also exercised compassion and the joy of giving, skills he will cherish.*

This simple Level 4 example illustrates how the freedom to experiment with facts—to play with them, challenge them, advance them into a personally meaningful context—drastically enhances the learner's experience. Thoughts now burn with the "fuel" of internal energy, and are guided by creative intelligence. The learner becomes an active participant, the most important ingredient of the learning process, instead of a mere passive receiver.

The main difference between Levels 1 through 3 and Level 4 can be boiled down to a single ingredient which family centered educators discover daily—learner interest.

> One group of researchers tried to sort out the factors that helped third and fourth graders remember what they had been reading. They found that how interested the students were in the passage was *thirty times* more important than how 'readable' the passage was.
>
> —Alfie Kohn in *Punished by Rewards*

At Level 4, activities are not prescribed ahead of time and assigned externally via a curriculum to produce certain skills. Rather, the same skills (or more) artfully emerge as the learner engages in activities of his own choosing. You might say, at the lower levels of the pyramid, skills are acquired—hopefully. At Level 4, skills are brought forth—naturally.

For those of you who may be skeptical (for I can totally understand your skepticism if you have never trusted a child to this degree), Jane M. Healy, Ph.D.'s *Endangered Minds* gracefully shares scientific evidence of Level 4 benefits in laymen's terms. After an interesting journey through the development of a human brain and the environmental impact on its formation, Healy summarizes the scientific evidence. "External pressure designed to produce learning or intelligence violates the fundamental rule: *A healthy brain stimulates itself by active interaction with what it finds challenging and interesting in its environment.*"[3]

Public school rarely, if ever, moves beyond Level 3. Using Levels 1—3, they seek to implant skills to serve the needs of the economic and political machinery. With close examination, you'll see these skills are grounded in conformity to a prescribed way of thinking and behaving. At Level 4, the skills brought forth *serve the learner*. They are, in fact, what I call "universal life skills." They pertain not to singular tasks, but are important, transferable skills the learner can bring to bear on dissimilar tasks in the future.

> You make a great, a very great mistake if you think that psychology, being the science of the mind's law, is something from which you can deduce definite programmes and schemes and methods of

instruction for immediate classroom use. Psychology is a science, and teaching is an art; and sciences never generate arts directly out of themselves. An intermediary inventive mind must make the application, by using its originality.

—William James, speaking to Cambridge, MA teachers (1892)

The implications of Level 5—Connection—are enormous. The apex of our Education Pyramid, Connection is an ideal not often reached, but the view from this summit is worth the effort to arrive.

Reaching Level 5 requires conscious awareness that goes beyond, or transcends, the "knowing" of normal, waking consciousness. This type of "knowing" is impossible to explain with words, for how can we verbalize or intellectualize something that exists beyond our senses and the relative field? A "relative world" understanding of the subject can be obtained with study, if you are interested enough. It is called (of course!) the science of consciousness, and here's a taste of it from Christopher Hills, Ph.D., author of *Nuclear Evolution*:

"The yogic science of consciousness lists three methods of validating knowledge. The first is knowledge of the knower or observer's limitations, leading to the study of ontology, the science of Being, which deals with the nature of perception. The second method deals with epistemology and is identical with what the West calls scientific method. The third method is transcendental knowing, which unites the previous two in the study of reason itself since, rationally, all effects must be traced to their causes, all perceptions traced to the perceiver, and all evidence examined from the point of view of the Universal Intelligence. This three-step validation enables the student of the knowing process to penetrate directly beyond the relative and comparative knowledge yielded by what we call the scientific method of validation."[4]

Hills and company are not the only scientists heading down this path. Gary Zukav, author of the layman's guide to physics, *The Dancing Wu Li Masters*, describes quantum physicists as a group saying, "We are not sure, but we have accumulated evidence which indicates that the key to understanding the universe is you."[5]

The more quantum physicists discover, the more unity they uncover, going as far as saying the physical world is "a web of relationships between elements whose meanings arise wholly from their relationships to the whole."[6] Today's exciting scientific study is rapidly moving toward the connection, the interaction, and the dependence between the observer and the observed, leading us naturally to the knower and the known.

The union of the knower and the known may be considered the ultimate vantage point from which to know anything. Much time must pass and many elements must fall together for this to materialize—energy, intelligence, learner interest, universal thinking skills and, of course, knowledge. Achievement is a tall order for anyone. But one thing is for sure: Neither creative intelligence nor internal energy find freedom to blossom under the shadow of teachers confined by their own conditioning, or under the oppression of pseudo-scientific education methods where method reigns more important than the individual.

If you plan, for your children's sake, to take responsibility for their education you're free to reach for the stars. And the peak of the Education Pyramid is worth stretching for.

> ...it makes sense for parents to consider putting aside grades and scores as indications of success and to look instead at the child's interest in learning. This is the primary criterion by which schools (and our own actions) should be judged.
>
> —Alfie Kohn in *Punished by Rewards*

CHAPTER FOUR

ADDICTED TO EXPERTS

Far from helping students to develop into mature, self-reliant, self-motivated individuals, schools seem to do everything they can to keep youngsters in a state of chronic, almost infantile, dependency. The pervasive atmosphere of distrust, together with rules covering the most minute aspects of existence, teach students every day they are not people of worth, and certainly not individuals capable of regulating their own behavior.

—Chas. E. Silberman in *Crisis in the Classroom*

Oh, if only the treatment described on the previous page were just happening to today's school kids! Then you, a clear-minded, self-reliant parent, could fix everything. You could change the environment your children are forced to endure ten months each year.

But it's not just happening to your kids today. The truth is, it's nothing new. (Silberman wrote his words in 1970!) The truth is, as you innocently skipped to school in days gone by, you were subject to the same treatment. Welcome to America, land of the self-doubters and home of twenty million "experts" ready and willing to continue where school left you off.

It stands to reason that if we parents were taught dependency on others, we are likely to feel very vulnerable when people waving college degrees and making livings in certain subject areas come along. We don't need to take responsibility for any of the dozens of things that go wrong in life. As long as we consult an expert (for s/he knows more than we), our troubles can be pigeon-holed and the expert can share his "secret formula" for fixing things. (After all, it has worked so well for countless others.) While in some cases this does make the initial trouble go away, what are the consequences of relinquishing responsibility this way?

Relying on "experts" to solve our problems leaves us feeling even *more* dependent on others, less self-assured of our ability to manage our own lives, and more likely to run to yet another "expert" in the future. Our immediate problem has vanished, but these side-effects of dependency never go away. Their shadows render us impotent in other aspects of our lives, leaving us unable to answer that simple question "who are you?", so alienated from our own feelings, thoughts, and choices do we become.

"High school students," reports Alfie Kohn, "accustomed to a highly directive style of instruction and suddenly asked to think for themselves, have been known to insist that *they have 'a right to be told what to do.'*"[1] (Emphasis added.)

"We have a right," our forefathers cried once upon a time, "to think for ourselves." We have surrendered that right, not to a dictatorial, hostile monarchy overseas, but to our own government's institutions. And oh, the tangled web these institutions have woven.

A web, because their "experts" pervade every area of our lives today. Tangled, because they work hand-in-hand. Woven, because they get closer to marriage every day we remain asleep.

It all begins in school, folks. By law, it is required that you attend. (That you learn is not required, that school be the best place for you to learn is not required, just that you attend.)

I'm going to repeat a paragraph from "Meet Your Makers." See if our little talk about experts sheds even more light on its significance now:

"School," says Ivan Illich, "prepares for the alienating institutionalization of life by teaching the need to be taught."[2] This way you may spend the rest of your life seeking out and paying others for thinking *you* are capable of doing, *if only you know that to be true.* But sadly, not too many people making a living in the education business are ready to teach themselves out of jobs. Furthermore, "Once a man or woman has accepted the need for school, he or she is easy prey for other institutions."[3]

When I speak of being asleep, my best argument for that statement is this: It's the only state we could possibly be in to have allowed the current state of affairs to exist! What other "excuse" could "justify" *what we ourselves have created by our acceptance and participation?*

The good part about having lent a hand in creating something is that it means you *have the capacity* to lend a hand in dis-creating it. That, my friends, is what they call the good news.

The bad news is that once you know something to be true, the only option you have, in good conscience (or awakened consciousness—they are the same thing) is action. As in the Talmudic Axiom "Let not thy learning exceed thy deeds. Mere knowledge is not the goal, but action." As in there ain't no turning back.

Now you are learning you *can* spare your children. You *can* wake up. You are the only one who *can* take action. Don't worry if your neighbor is "taking action." Don't worry about what the neighbors might think about you "taking action." Individuals have to come to this point of their own free will, in whatever way it happens. You can live your life as an example. Others will see it.

This is how family centered education started; individuals taking action on behalf of their own children. And new families begin every day—after reading a book, speaking with a neighbor, attending a local gathering on the subject, catching TV coverage of other families, or good ol' fashioned soul-searching.

They have, all in their own way, decided to raise their children without the help of education "experts:" teachers, educational textbook publishers, administrators, school psychologists, curricula writers (for the "normal," for the "gifted," for the "disadvantaged"), PTA, or the National Education Association (NEA) and its state unions.

They have, all in their own way, been succeeding very nicely.

I wish I could report that somehow family centered education has managed to grow and thrive without its share of "experts," but I can't. I don't know at what point we reached critical mass, but we have become "a market." Our mailboxes overflow with advertisements, post card sales packets, announcements, catalogs, curriculum deals, computer flyers and work-at-home deals. Everyone, it seems, has something to sell us. Some of the products are wonderful; some of them would be better left as shade for spotted owls.

The most destructive sales pitches come from those claiming to be (what else?) "homeschool experts." How anyone can hawk curricula and preach that he has "the way" to homeschool, claiming all the while that he understands family centered education, is beyond me. But these people keep on selling—and selling very well.

It's not surprising. Many of us arrive at our decision to "skip school" with our "schooled" mind. We bring to this new experience the fruits of our own past experience of learning, which most often are subjects, class periods, desks, chalkboards, text books, curriculum, etc. As has become our habit, we look outside ourselves for an "expert" to tell us what to do.

So eager-to-make-money "experts" jump to your rescue. They understand—and use—humankind's most powerful emotions and vulnerabilities. When it comes to leaving the comfort of what is known (traditional school) and stepping out into the unknown (family centered education), "experts" focus on these three:

1) Ignorance—I don't know what I'm doing; I'm not smart enough; what if I don't cover everything the school system wants me to cover?; I never understood math; can learning *really* be different than what I remember?
2) Greed—I want my child to be the best; I want my child to have the most; I want my child to win a Nobel Prize; I want my child to make a lot of money; I want, I want, I want...
3) Fear—If you don't do it legally you could go to jail; if you do it legally you could still go to jail; don't mingle with the heathens; what if I do a lousy job?; what if the school administrators aren't cooperative?; what if, what if, what if...

Full of self-doubt and dependence-oriented, people buy just about anything that comes with a promise of success. These "experts," though, merely perpetuate "school-at-home" instead of freeing individuals to explore new paths in learning. This is the greatest harm they inflict on more families than I care to count.

When it comes to your child, who has the most current and intimately informed connection? It's you, of course. And aren't up-to-date and well-informed folks in any field called "experts?"

Consider yourself the most qualified person when it comes to choosing what's best for your family. Be wary of the "expert" who professes to know what's right for you. You may want to use the following criteria in evaluating the usefulness of any opinion, product, or service presented to you:

Motivation

Why is this expert helping you? Does s/he have a hidden agenda? Some family centered learning "experts" preach a personal doctrine, intent on generating power through a "following." Their followers usually conform to a narrow standard of belief set forth by the leaders of the organization, creating an unspoken but very real intolerance of anyone whose views differ from their own. It is hard, indeed, to establish self-control and freedom in your child's education if all you do is trade one set of "experts" for another.

Is the expert helping you at a large profit to himself? There's nothing wrong with somebody making a buck. But if this expert draws you into a no cost/low cost seminar, then tells you there is only one right way to teach your kids—and he just happens to sell a complete $2000 kit that fits the bill—run to the nearest exit! Real education need not be expensive or packaged. In fact, the more freedom you employ while picking and choosing materials based on your child's educational interests, the more likely your child will be successful.

Make sure any major purchases truly fill your family's needs and are in keeping with your personal philosophy. It's one thing to blow $15 on a book you decide not to read, but quite another to spend ten times as much on a dozen books and scores of worksheets that you wind up giving away at your next garage sale! Ask to purchase an inexpensive sampling of materials so you can put them to the test. See if the kids get motivated by the content *and* the approach.

Allow yourself a "cool-down" period after a seminar or sales talk and let your initial excitement wear off. A rightly motivated "expert" will want your child to benefit from the materials at any point. If it's truly a good deal, it should still be around a week or a month or even a year later.

Approach

Does the "expert" respect you as a thinking person, or does he write or speak as if his opinion came down from the mountain with Moses? The way an "expert" conveys his message reveals a lot about his motivation. Beware the "preacher," telling you what is good or bad for your child. That's your call, remember?

There are many experienced, capable folks who don't bill themselves as "experts," yet they share excellent insights into family centered learning in a casual, relaxed manner. They readily admit "their way" is not for everyone, and you walk away from their seminars feeling as if you just spent the afternoon with a good friend. They offer suggestions and personal experience in lieu of mandates. And if you buy their wares, they are grateful and hope they work as well for you as they have for them.

Value

Is the "expert's" opinion or material really worthwhile? This, of course, is a judgment call. As a general rule, the harder the sell, the more closely you should examine the offer. Don't just buy the sizzle; make sure there's some meat attached. Hold the "expert" to any promises, explicit or implied.

Is the great new phonics program merely a collection of tired ol' worksheets? Could you spend five minutes each day and put together the same collection of first grade addition problems to drill your child if that, in fact, is what you really want? Will your kids get excited and play that history game more than once? Materials, as well as opinions, are only valuable if you can put them to good use.

Results

Are you and your child comfortable and happy with this approach to learning? Does the "expert's" method work? Do you see growth and real learning taking place with these materials?

You don't need a battery of tests to determine the results of learning experiences. If it's a positive experience, your child remains interested and excited. He talks about what he learns, not just to share it with you, but also to internalize the new-found knowledge. He asks additional questions and notices when the subject appears in conversation, on TV or in written materials.

If the experience is a negative one, he'll complain or ask to do something—anything!—else. Most kids will let you know, in no uncertain terms, that the subject matter OR the presentation of the information is irrelevant to their experience. In short, they turn off.

And what about you, as teacher and guide? An approach that's right for you should empower you, filling you with confidence and a "can do" attitude. On the other hand, if an "expert's" advice leaves you feeling less than whole, or dependent on either his message or methods, watch out. Someone's getting empowered. And it's not you.

You can be much more than a passive spectator when it comes to the "experts." Do some detective work before plunking down good money on what may prove worthless to your family. Ask other family centered learners if they have had any experience with the "expert." If so, find out just what they received from the encounter, always remembering, of course, that what is good for the Jones' may not be best for you.

If there is no one nearby who can help you, request references directly from the "expert" or his company. It's always better to talk to someone who has attended a seminar or used the product than to rely purely on ads. Investing a few dollars in phone calls before the plunge could save you a lot of travel time, money, disappointment, and/or aggravation.

With the remarkably diverse backgrounds and reasons parents bring to family centered learning, no one method and no one person's opinions satisfy everyone. After everyone has had his say, let go of that feeling of chronic, almost infantile, dependency. Trust yourself to decide what is best for you and your family.

CHAPTER FIVE

BIRDS DON'T GO TO FLIGHT SCHOOL

ARTIFICIAL LEARNING VS NATURAL EDUCATION

Let us never forget that the law is adaption to circumstances, be they what they may. And if, rather than allow men to come in contact with the real circumstances of their position, we place them in artificial—in false—circumstances, they will adapt themselves to these instead; and will, in the end, have to undergo the miseries of a readaption to the real ones.

—Herbert Spencer in *Social Statics*

I f you love *any* child, you are well aware of our society's precarious position regarding our children. With all the promise of modern technology to keep them physiologically healthier than any previous generation, we are losing our youngsters in record number to street violence, drugs, and AIDS, reflecting a general disregard for the beauty and sanctity of this gift we call Life.

What good is the promise of longer life if, in the formative, previously hope-filled years of adolescence, our youth decide that Life is worth less than a temporary high, a ten-minute ride in a stolen car, or the cost of a pair of sneakers?

How have our children arrived at this place? How did the quality of life for millions of young citizens deteriorate so dramatically, so quickly? What happened to our forefathers' promise of life, liberty, and the pursuit of happiness for all?

There are no easy answers to any of these questions. Each question can—and does—fill book after book with statistics, facts, and conclusions each author hopes can restore sanity to a nation whose young inhabitants grow more and more disturbed each day. While these authors expend precious time and brain power tinkering with the current educational system (which crystallizes our approach to life and learning), most fail to uncover the true cause, the catalyst that sends our children seeking meaning, connection, respect and love from the least likely places.

I'd like you to take a few moments, sit back and relax, and remember your formative years. Any of your teenage time will do. Remember what was personally important to you; think about your environment—your neighborhood, school, friends, teachers, your relationship with your parents; recall your favorite TV show, commercial, songs, movies.

You probably felt the threat of the Cold War, but it remained in the shadows, never materializing. You knew the neighbors knew your parents and wouldn't hesitate to report any mischief you created. Teachers worried about students chewing gum and talking in class. Many times Mom waved good-bye as you left for school, and greeted you upon your return. Keeping up with the world was easy—just pick one of three half-hour news programs. A favorite TV show tickled your funny bone or sent your imagination flying. It was a very different time, wasn't it?

Now spend a few minutes reflecting on life for a teen today. The threat of annihilation comes not from faceless, nameless Soviets far away, but from the kid who sits in front of history class or the guy that hangs on the corner or a passing car. Neighbors don't know each other's names, and scurry to safety when the neighborhood kids "act up." A National School Boards Association survey released in January, 1994, found that of the 729 school districts reporting, 60% saw student assaults on teachers. Mom has to earn a living, and may not send her kids off to school *or* greet them afterwards. Fast and furiously changing world news and maps confront us from scores of TV stations, and wars—across the world or down the street—unfold before a child's eyes. Favorite TV shows depict countless scenes of violence and destruction or humor that revolves around vivid sexual innuendo, revenge, or insult-hurling. Government sponsored condom commercials blink on and off between ads using sex to sell anything our materialistic little hearts could desire. (Talk about mixed messages, messages targeted to a population fixated on their ripening sexuality. Remember?)

As we sleep, the world and existence changes; whether for better or worse is not to be debated here. Because of these changes, we've increased the demands on our children. They're growing up faster and faster trying to keep up, but we've done absolutely nothing to increase their ability, their intelligence, or even their desire to handle these demands. To make matters worse, we're leaving their emotional coattails exposed, blowing helter-skelter at the whim of every societal breeze.

Change outpaced our schools' ability to keep up. Using teaching methods suited for providing basic skills in the nineteenth century, we ask students staring down the twenty-first century to ingest more and more information—while leaving the heart behind.

Since compulsory schooling began, we've seen a scientific revolution in our understanding of how humans learn, yet schools continue to plod along using the same bland text books, the I preach/you listen approach to learning, and the same "judgment by grade and class position."

Technology invades every aspect of job and work yet fails to appear in many classrooms. When technology does show up, short class periods and long user lines effectively separate individual students from meaningful exploration of its potential.

Times change. Schools don't. That's part of artificial learning.

Off the top of my head, I can't think of another species besides human beings that separates a child from its parents when she's ready to acquire life skills. Because our society accepts artificial learning as the norm, it looks at natural education (or family centered education) as abnormal when, in truth, it is the popular, accepted way to learn that is synthetic.

Birds don't go to flight school. It's Momma standing there when baby first sets sail across the tree tops. Momma teaches babies to hunt for food, and to find or build a shelter. In short, Momma teaches baby Life. Not *about* Life. Life itself. This is natural education.

Our society says: Only trained professionals who have read enough books and listened to enough lectures and taken enough tests may teach our children. They, in turn, read books *about* life with the assembly of children gathered into a special building, isolated from the community—an institution. It's impossible to teach Life itself in the confines of an institutional setting. Anyone who has ever been inside a hospital, prison, military base, school, or college can tell you—the institution is a world unto itself.

You may argue that a robin, for example, has much less to teach her child about life than you. She teaches the basics—robin style— and she teaches them in a much shorter period of time.

Teaching life takes longer for us humans because of all the wonderful complexities of our mind and spirit. We are social beings, so lessons go beyond survival to getting along with our fellow beings. But just because it takes longer, does that mean the job should be handed over to another?

When we pass responsibility for educating our children to others, and send them all off to an institution to do it, we place Life in an artificial context. Thus, any learning that happens to come as a result is, at best, irrelevant; at worst, perverted. Artificial learning takes what is simple and natural and turns it into a complex array of objectives, goals, measurements, administrators, supervisors, counselors, and transportation experts. Natural education requires only a guide providing direction, and a learner ready to discover and create goals and values that are personally meaningful.

Artificial learning seeks to permeate us from somewhere outside of ourselves. It doesn't strengthen the foundation that already exists, but attempts to attach extensions, no matter the condition of the base. Information pours into our heads, then pours back out to make sure some of it hit its mark. Information received like this is not part of our personal experience of life, so it cannot possibly translate into improvement of our lives. Instead, it works to convince us that our lives improve only as *we* change to measure up to criteria set forth in somebody else's goals.

> *There was just enough room for the guidance counselor and me to sit at either side of the desk among the filing cabinets and stacks of catalogs and papers.*
>
> *"It's time to finish planning your Senior year," said Mrs. Case as she surveyed my ever-thickening file. "You need to choose one more elective course. What would you like?"*
>
> *"Put me down for Home Economics," I answered.*
>
> *"Linda," said Mrs. Case looking over the rim of her glasses, "You need courses that challenge you on your transcript." She took the list from my hands and scanned the contents.*
>
> *"Modern European History looks good, and colleges seem to like it," she said to the paper.*
>
> *I swallowed. "O.K."*
>
> *The only thing I remember from Modern European History is that the Battle of Hastings was fought in 1066. I don't remember why. I fell in love instead of going to college. I've cooked and sewn daily for two decades.*

If we change to fit others' goals for us, we sense we are powerless behind a mask that hides our true nature. Eventually, we forget our original face. If we don't change, labels follow us through our learning careers—troublemaker, learning disabled, special needs, hyperactive, *ad nauseam.*

Natural learning guides us back to true education. We sharpen the abilities our children already possess—Curiosity, Imagination, Creativity, Inner Peace, Humor, Artistry, Self-Motivation, and Intuition—which become the best tools to learn anything, anytime.

When a child *wants* to learn, she is *ready* to learn. No need for threats, rewards, or punishments in the form of bad grades or humiliation to get her going. You need only be awake enough and observant enough to recognize an interest. Then seize the moment. Her Curiosity will drive her to open the book on the subject you happen to leave on the coffee table. Self-motivation leads her to ask if you can take her to the library or a neighbor to find out more. Creativity, Imagination and Artistry allow her to bring all that she has absorbed into concrete form, be it in the shape of a story, a drawing, a thoughtful question, or the entire next week's theme during playtime.

These moments show us the point of learning is not to memorize facts for a test tomorrow, nor to pull them out of a hat ten years from now. It's to realize learning has its own value, *as is*.

Let's examine the message we send our kids about what aspect of life we consider valuable when we practice artificial learning. A flurry of activity precedes the start of school in September. TV commercials and newspaper ads blast the message, "It's time to get ready!" New clothes, shoes, notebooks, pens, paper, lunchbox; this must be important! The family's schedule revolves around the bus timetable and school hours which, not coincidentally, bear a remarkable resemblance to job hours. Children rush out the door reminded that school—and doing well in it—is serious stuff.

The better part of each day for the better part of each year is spent getting to school, attending school, and doing school work at home. Although there's usually a nice buffet of electives so older children can "spice up" their day, the basics usually run something like this: math, science, history, geography, and English. Other requirements—music, art, health, and physical education—appear on most curricula, but usually receive attention on a weekly, rather than a daily, basis.

This is all "head" work, intellectual stimulation (if the kids are lucky!) day in and day out. While Imagination may occasionally spread its wings in English class creative writing or a forty-five minute art period once a week, the final products, reviewed and graded and criticized, remain the property of the intellectual realm.

The child poet learns he must first master proper grammar and spelling, understand alliteration, and read the complete works of Shakespeare, to the teacher's satisfaction, before his deepest feelings can be appreciated. By the time he swallows all of this and learns to outmaneuver the red pen, desire to express deep feelings disappears. The child scientist, curious about how the world and its vast array of possibilities works, leaves enthusiasm on a back burner until he memorizes the dates of previous discoveries, watches the life extinguished from a living animal so he can cut it open, and reads others' theories in ten year-old textbooks. He forgets the questions that once fueled his days.

This approach would work if human beings were nothing more than giant intellects roaming the earth. But we also have hands, connected to the brain via nerves, that need to touch, to build, to create. Babies and toddlers, those wonderful little creatures who learn to talk and walk without manuals and college-educated trainers, feel and explore everything in their path. Perfect examples of the power of inner drive in action, young children satisfy their hunger using this particular brand of sensory input to make sense of their world.

> *The brand new gumball machine sits empty atop the refrigerator. With half the family already out the door on the way to an appointment, the three year-old eagerly eyes the machine. "I want gum, please."*
>
> *"Here," says Mom reaching into the box of gumballs on the counter. "You can take two."*
>
> *Stomping his foot, the three year-old shouts, "No, I want THAT gum," as he points to the machine.*
>
> *Mom removes the lid and pours gumballs until the machine's globe glistens with a rainbow of colors. The child already holds a penny retrieved from the coin jar. He waits patiently.*
>
> *In goes the penny. Out pops a gumball.*
>
> *"I have one and it's a green one, right, Mommy?" the child asks as he turns the door knob.*
>
> *Mom smiles. "It is one. It is green." She closes the door behind her.*

It is not natural—even if we accept it as normal—to lose this drive with age. Except in those few rare birds who somehow escape and survive as our artists and craftspeople, years of programming to set exploration aside in favor of book learning buries our drive. It's still there, unfulfilled and withering.

Human beings have a bridge linking the internal world to the external. We call it heart. Through this aspect of humanness we feel and express emotion. It allows us to fill poetry and music and paintings and sculpture with meaning. It allows us connection with fellow human beings. When we serve others who need our time and help, it is because this ground has been tended, nurtured, and prepared to receive the seed of empathy.

The internal world houses intuition, a vast storehouse of knowledge gathered over time. Intuition waits for our intellect to get out of the way so it may guide and serve us. It waits patiently, and will not speak at all if we don't know how to listen.

Is it any wonder our children are failing to achieve in school? They must sense, at some deep, intuitive place, that they are being short-changed. Artificial education's focus on intellect and its accompaniments—job, money, fame, power—throws them off-balance. Learning how to read, write, work with numbers and understand our world and its history are essential—but they're not all that is essential.

When we place all the weight on one side of an airplane, it cannot soar smoothly. When we place all importance on a child's intellect, as artificial learning does, he cannot soar smoothly, either. We make his flight toward independence unnecessarily difficult and dangerous. If we shift the plane's weight, we achieve equilibrium. Only when we pay equal attention to all aspects of a child, when *we* value his hands and heart equally with his head, will he achieve symmetry. Then watch him fly!

In *The Conflict in Education in a Democratic Society*, Robert Hutchins told us, "Society is to be improved, not by forcing a program of social reform down its throat, through the schools or otherwise, but by the improvement of the individuals who compose it."

Artificial learning situations don't give us opportunity for this type of improvement because advancement of the individual and his unique potential are not their goal. The only thing that has improved in compulsory schooling's history is its ability to absorb ever larger amounts of tax dollars. About the only place the individual counts is in the bottom line, for his presence equals thousands of dollars of federal, state, and local monies pouring into the coffers. If the "individual" happens to wear a label like learning disabled or gifted, and is said to require "special" education, so much the better—he's worth even more.

Without massive sums of money, where would the education system be? Would local property owners provide rent-free learning space? Would publishers contribute books because they know the books are improving society? Would administrators daily arrive because of a heart-felt knowledge that their work improves the quality of life in homes and communities? Would teachers teach for the personal satisfaction the act provides?

Silly questions? On the surface, yes. But let's alter one small point in the above scenario. Instead of money, what if education is motivated by love?

Suddenly "improvement of the individual" takes center stage. The individual, not the system, is the main concern. Instead of being the source of income, each student discovering his potential is the source, period.

Maybe this attention will never reach every child everywhere. But it is key to the success of "home" schools. When education is directed with love instead of driven by money, our questions aren't silly anymore. In fact, family centered educators can answer yes to all of them!

Many state laws limit you to offering rent-free learning space only to your own children, but that's OK. You know what they say about smaller class size—it's better for everyone.

Publishers don't go around "contributing" books, *per se*. But when asked, they do offer discounts. This is not to say they are then cheap. Get yourself a real education by reading a few educational supply catalogs and check out the prices: Fifteen minute video cassettes, ranging from poor to excellent in quality and educational value, can cost up to $69.95! One support group got a distributor to knock 33% right off the top just by asking. Support groups purchase and share materials too, cutting the cost per family. Many evolve into resource centers providing increasingly interesting and unique opportunities to their communities.

The "administrators" and "teachers" in our new scenario are, of course, you. You're an administrator working because you want to, not because the paycheck pays the bills. No unions, no strikes, no school board politics, no state aid to be justified so that next year's donation is at least as large. Just someone who cares deeply about a child's future.

You choose the role of teacher (and I hope you quickly discover there are dozens of ways beyond our traditional approach to accomplish your goals) because of love for your students. Little do you realize at first how much learning, how much joy lies ahead for you, too. Your journey as teacher, guiding with love, connects you to your own inner abilities and draws them out, even as you guide your children. No tenure, no cost-of-living raises, no student assaults on teachers, no guns or drugs in the "classroom," and a real shot at our forefathers' promise of life, liberty, and the pursuit of happiness for all.

This is natural education. Education stripped of all that keeps *it* from reaching its potential—an insatiable appetite for money, a layer of administration thick enough to smother any size institution, government control via regulations and funds, and unionization. This is family centered education.

I trust that were we to offer the balance and purity available in natural education as a steady diet to our children, they'd finish everything on their plates and come back for more. Balanced learning with loved ones provides that sense of wholeness it is our nature to seek. Instead of feeling denied, we feel fulfilled. Instead of feeling disrespected, we respect Self. Instead of separation, we experience connection.

To be the best, happiest people we can be, humans need connection on an intimate level as well as on a broader, community level. Gangs and early sexual experiences look like our kids' answer to the missing sense of family, fulfilling the intimate need. And the most accessible answers to a sense of community, at least to the economic community of choice (remember, we hammer the message of money's connection to happiness into our kids) are drugs and violence. They certainly look like the straightest line from being nobody with nothing to being perceived as somebody with something. If fulfillment can't be found, temporarily full pockets will do. If not respect, a reputation. Apathy leading to violence against another or one's self is the shortest route to total disconnection, when the pain and emptiness surrounding Life make severing remaining ties the merciful choice.

ASSOCIATED PRESS NEWS REPORT

Mom: Boys Killed Selves Over School
Capital Times, Madison, WI, September 1, 1993, Excerpted.

A woman whose 10- and 13- year-old sohs died of gunshots...says
they evidently sneaked out of the house and killed themselves
rather than go to school...
"...They just hated school...
"...They wanted me to homeschool them. If I had only known it
was that important, I would have tried..."

With the status quo our culture grows increasingly illiterate,
unhappy, and hostile. If artificial learning creates, contributes to,
or in any way supports our children's sense of disconnection, it
cannot be healthy for us as individuals or as a society. If we just
left our kids alone, they'd have a better shot at discovering happiness and literacy in their own way. With family centered education, you are there as guide. You can ensure that balance permeates your children's experience of Life.

Save your flight school money. If bird-brain Momma robins can
keep their species alive and thriving in an increasingly adverse
environment, we can do the same for our children.

CHAPTER SIX

AS YOU SOW
SO SHALL YOU REAP

The only reason I always try to meet and know the parents better is because it helps me to forgive their children.

—Louis Johannot, Headmaster
Institut LeRosey, Switzerland

A young Japanese student on his way to an all-American Halloween party with a friend walks up to the wrong house. "Freeze!" the homeowner cries. The Japanese fellow doesn't understand. He doesn't "freeze." He dies.

His countrymen take classes before traveling to the United States. They learn what "freeze" means, they're told to hand money over to muggers and, by the time class is over, they know a midnight stroll on an American boulevard may be their last.

News stories on violence in American streets give way to reports on violence in the American workplace which make room for accounts of violence in American schools. 130,000 kids take guns to school every day. Juvenile arrests for murder climbed 85% in four years from 1987 to 1991.[1] Thanks to the Menendez brothers, parents across America are rearranging the furniture so they can see TV and keep an eye on the door at the same time.

Your children live in a violent, violent society wondering when, not if, catastrophe will pierce their lives. (America's approximately 250 million citizens have to dodge an overwhelming 220 million firearms[2].) This is a time of much fear and anger related, in part, to the ever-widening gap between the haves and have-nots, the stress generated by our conditioned way of life, and the symptoms of this stress—domestic violence, drug and alcohol use, and the emotional and psychic imbalance that are the legitimate outcome of ignoring family and human nature.

America wasn't always like this. The problems of anger and violence, once a phenomena somewhere "out there," now penetrate most every average citizen's world. Anger and violence's cousin—corruption—infiltrates the lives of those with power, real or perceived. Had we not been lulled to sleep with our conditioning, we might have seen and stopped them before they infected our children—maybe.

But we, the well-programmed people, turned to our institutions and said, "Government—DO something. Schools—DO something!"

And they did.

They said, "Families, since you've an obvious need to make money (It's all right, dear, everyone has the same problem.), take your babies to day care centers. We'll prepare your children for future institutionalization while they're in preschool. Since you don't have the time, we'll feed them breakfast. We'll teach them about sex and drugs. We'll create special classes to "teach" values. We'll train them to be good citizens. We'll route them into a career. We'll act *in loco parentis* (in place of parents)." And they did it *their* way.

Alarm bells should have gone off at least twelve years ago when *A Nation at Risk* outlined the poor job schools were doing in reading, writing and arithmetic. If "it's an insane tragedy that 700,000 people get a diploma each year and can't read the damned diploma,"[3] what made us believe schools were doing any better *in loco parentis* ?

"We seem, as a nation, to be drifting toward a new concept of childhood which says that a child can be brought into this world and allowed to fend for himself or herself," said U.S. Secretary of Education Richard Riley in February, 1994's first State of American Education address. "There is a disconnection here that demands our attention...a disconnection so pervasive between adult America and the children of America that we are all losing touch with one another."

Schools condition adults (parents) to raise capital instead of kids. Parents disconnect from kids. Schools take over even more parenting responsibilities. Parents disconnect further from kids. Schools call in social services to repair the trauma. Parents disconnect even further from kids. Schools do even more of what they already do. And then those children have children.

> I cannot help but wonder whether by continuing and expanding the school lunch program, we aren't witnessing, if not encouraging, the slow demise of yet another American tradition: the brown bag...
>
> Perhaps we are beholding yet another break in the chain that links child to home.
>
> —Chas. McC. Mathias, Jr., U.S. Senator, *Time*, August 16, 1976

We allow our institutions to sow the seeds we ourselves should plant in our children's lives. It is up to parents to plant the seeds of trust and respect as children stretch to define Self. Instead we let schools sow self-doubt, defining your child's life according to an authoritarian checklist over which she has no control.

When children's lives call for connection, wholeness and inner peace, nurtured in large part through cooperative acts, schools sow the seed of competition.

When it's time for parents to sow and nurture self-motivation and self-responsibility, the institution plants the "External Control Brothers," or reward and punishment, in their place.

The remaining important seeds in a parent's bag—curiosity, imagination, creativity, and intuition—never reach fertile ground, for tests cover our children's lives in their stead. No need for creativity when there's only one right answer. No need for curiosity or imagination when a day is full of busy work concocted by others. No need for intuition when you think the outer world holds all significance.

You might think that all these negative seeds are more than enough to accomplish the children's surrender to the will of the institution, readying them to serve their vital role on the economic merry-go-round. But for good measure (and the "perks" associated with the commodity), schools fertilize the ground with ever-increasing amounts of... advertising.

> Now you can enter the classroom through custom-made learning materials created with your specific marketing objectives in mind. Communicate with young spenders directly and, through them, their teachers and families as well.
> —From Lifetime Learning Systems
> (educational software company) promo in *Advertising Age*

Perhaps one thought from an *Advertising Age* essay best captures how completely we surrender responsibility for our kids. While we sleep advertisers create "brand and product loyalties through *classroom-centered, peer-powered lifestyle patterning.*" [4] (Emphasis added.)

By allowing the institutions to choose which seeds to sow, parents have no control over what blossoms. By denying our time and attention during the growing season, parents don't supervise the growing environment. By refusing to weed, water, and tend to daily nurturing toward a healthy harvest, parents have no right to expect a job well done.

So what do we reap in place of wholesome life?

Instead of acting as responsible gardeners and planting trust and respect, we surrender our children's time to schools where self-doubt seeds (labels, tests, grades, surveillance, etc.) bear the ugly fruit of low-esteem, dependence, and a mistaken belief that individuals are not responsible for their actions. While Nature is gently, constantly, urging children toward independence, their external world, including the adults they depend on, is preparing them for slavery. Conflict—internal *and* external—arises, and the fruit's perfume floats across the land: American Anger.

> The problem is fundamental. Put 20 or more children of roughly the same age in a little room, confine them to desks, make them wait in line, make them behave. It is as if a secret committee, now lost to history, had made a study of children and, having figured out what the greatest number were least disposed to do, declared that all of them should do it.
> —Tracy Kidder in *Among Schoolchildren*

The institution's seed of competition grows fruit larger than watermelons—selfishness and disregard for the happiness or success of "competitors." Learned disregard for others creates too much shade for light-loving compassion to grow. Instead of connection to people, children find separation and the loneliness that suicide "heals." Those who keep going fill the emptiness by connecting to the "things" they've been taught to revere, now so important to the "good life" it matters not how they are obtained. The perfume, violence, grows nauseatingly stronger each day.

> I sure as hell didn't mean for people to crush human values and morality.
> —Vince Lombardi on his much more often quoted comment "Winning isn't everything: it's the only thing."

The institution has reward and punishment seeds. The plants that emerge sport thorns and long, dark, twisted vines of resentment and irreverence. If a child is hearty enough, resistance will also grow. More concerned with obedience than healthy growth, schools use reward and punishment seeds for crowd management, devastated by the ugly fruit they produce yet ignorant of their role in its production.

Reward and punishment as incentives just may be the most bitter seeds planted in your child's life at school, for they teach the fine art of cunning manipulation.   One who has experienced manipulation holds the most potential for becoming a master manipulator himself. (Ever watched an older child applying this useful tool with a younger one? The learned behavior may be used in an apparently harmless way as bribing a sibling to leave the room or keep a secret from Mom, or advance to juvenile criminal activity when kids extort lunch money from frightened underclassmen.)

He who learns the game well holds a most powerful key to the psychological control of fellow human beings—every one has his price, and it's only a matter of finding the *right* carrot or stick to do the job. Because selfishness, irresponsibility for actions and separation have also taken root, and the "exceptional" student becomes cunning enough to use the same game that was used on him, the perfume of reward and punishment wafts all the way from crack houses to police stations, from street gangs to the military, from rural town halls to Washington, D. C. This pungent perfume is called corruption.

> No system really works unless it operates with incentives.
> —Albert Shanker, President of the American Federation of
> Teachers

So anger, violence, and corruption permeate our society. Not a single aspect of life goes untouched. But then not a single word of blame can be thrown, either. Parents sleep beneath their quilt of conditioning, schools continue sewing new quilts all the time. When it comes to accepting responsibility for children, nobody is home.

Cheating in military academies. Child abuse. Hazing activities carried to extremes. Drugs. Twenty-five million Americans, almost half of them under 17, using food pantries and soup kitchens. Guns. Car-jackings. Alcohol. An epidemic of political scandal. Teen pregnancy. Trade wars. Real wars. One in every sixty-five citizens are in jail, on parole, or are ex-cons.[5] Suicide.

Bigotry. Domestic violence. American spies in Russia. Chinese spies in America. And weapons stolen from National Guard posts sold by Guardsmen and others on the streets, providing the ultimate irony: We, the internally-conflicted people, have taken to pointing our government's weapons at ourselves.

> Our greatest moral problem today is cowardice. Common integrity now passes for courage.
>
> —Rev. Wm. Sloane Coffin, Jr.

U.S. Secretary of Education Richard Riley's address hits the nail of parental irresponsibility squarely on the head. But until he's ready to whack his own thumb with the hammer, too, institutionalized education reform will not improve our society. Public schooling—the system, the institution, the scientific methods of behavior control and modification—is rendering parents impotent. Impotent parents not only *want* to believe the schools are covering the parents' bases, they *have* to believe, regardless of the evidence to the contrary. Schoolmen can holler that the American family is breaking up and its members are isolating themselves from each other, but the institution must accept that its actions lead families toward these consequences, just as the alcoholic must realize his role in his problem before repair can begin. Like the alcoholic, schoolmen must know that the true work necessary today can't come from top-down *or* bottom-up; it must come from the inside of all individuals who play a part in raising children. The work must begin inside all of us.

Until an observer can look at our culture and say we have created human loyalties through family centered, parent (adult)-powered lifestyle patterning, we will all suffer consequences, from the senior-citizen afraid to walk outside after dusk to the newborn destined for institutional care before she sees her first month birthday.

Scientists call it cause and effect; Hindus call it karma; Christ said, "As you sow, so shall you reap." Whatever you call it, it is natural law. Natural law, you understand, bends for no one. Even with God in the Trinity of economy-dominated, government schools, they won't create a kinder, gentler nation or whole, happy individuals. Purposefully sowing seeds that produce anger, violence and corruption mutilates the human spirit, leaving us all too willing to accept disconnection from family, community, and self.

Author's Note: Once you realize this simple truth, the appealing idea of reclaiming responsibility for your own life and your child's education from the State is merely a matter of changing priorities. Let's spend a little time examining yours.

CHAPTER SEVEN

EXAMINING PRIORITIES

One cannot exist today as a person—One cannot exist in full consciousness—without having to have a showdown with one's self, without having to define what it is that one lives by, without being clear in one's own mind what matters and what does not matter.

—Dorothy Thompson, Columnist

From a 1939 speech

I chose Dorothy's quote to open this chapter, in part because her advice is as sound today as it was in 1939. Also, her words capture well the message that must be understood by parents who want to reclaim self and family. As you continue sending your child to the local school "because it's there," your family tosses about like a leaf in a windstorm, exposed to education's theoretical typhoons, intrusive government gales, economic monsoons and fateful societal tornadoes. If followed, Dorothy's advice provides your family an anchor, for only through a clear understanding of Self and what matters in life can you stand against the prevailing winds, holding fast to your ideals and sparing your family the hopelessness and fear of not knowing where they will be blown tomorrow.

Besides sharing the realities of education in our current society and the joy and benefits of family centered learning, I consider this a most important chapter of this book. Each of us can easily recognize the priorities of individual days, be they final arguments in a major court trial or getting a daughter's costume ready in time for tonight's premiere. The trouble is we bury ourselves in this day-to-day activity, foregoing the time to think about—let alone consciously assume control of—the actions which direct our lives. Our actions (and our pocket organizers), it turns out, control us.

Accomplishing all those "little" things appears a useless waste of time if we lose sight of the "big" things that are our true measure as human beings. If you sense something is missing from your family's life, rest assured you are not alone. Many of us don't take the next step and start asking questions because schooling trained us only to answer them. Many of us don't search for answers because schooling trained us to believe there is only *one* right answer. If we don't hit on that one immediately, we will wait until Jamaica freezes over for someone to tell us what that right answer is.

Your society's institutions tell you they have the right answer, the perfect game, and it permeates your subconscious all through your schooling years. *Spend your childhood learning to work. Work. Work harder.* Buy things; that's what's missing in your family's life.

With parents working endless hours in blind trust of that answer, there's no time to realize that "not even designer toys substitute for good-quality conversation."[1]

Right under our noses the price of our dream home doubled, tripled, quadrupled. One working parent per household wasn't enough. In March, 1994, CBS News reporter Ray Brady added another dose of reality: "Fortunate" Americans with jobs are working one month per year more today than twenty-five years ago just to hold on. *Work. Work harder. Every able body work!*

So moms and never-to-be moms entered the work force with astonishing speed. There was no time to ask "is this really what's best for our family?" or to examine the consequences of these actions for our relationships with children and spouse: The price of houses keeps climbing! We buy our houses (keeping those new construction figures up and the economy growing), never realizing that our personal economic achievements, as noticed by cultural observer Christopher Lasch, "undermine equally important values associated with the family...Feminists have not answered the argument that day care provides no substitute for the family...that *indifference to the needs of the young* has become one of the distinguishing characteristics of a society that lives for the moment."[2] (Emphasis added.)

The game continues. Move up fast. Play hard. Keep your options open. Don't commit. Make more money to buy the new, improved "dream house:" got to have a sauna (oh, that job stress!), redwood deck (great for entertaining new money, I mean, clients), electronic alarm system (you've so many things to protect!), higher taxes for better schools for the kids (more money means better, right?). My, but that old dream house tarnished quickly, didn't it, dear? *Work harder. Every able body work! Indifference to the needs of the young.*

Our social institutions' answer is a one-way street to monopolization of family time. Systematically eating away family time around the edges—through school and an ever-escalating need and desire for more money—the institutions effectively prevent this essential element your family needs to function as a unit, a whole, a stable "home base" to which youngsters may return for necessary and frequent guidance, nurturance, love and acceptance. The institutions' answer directs us away from life, liberty and the pursuit of happiness toward possessions, corporate slavery and the pursuit of the almighty dollar. Lack of time together leads us to indifference to human connection, compassion, cooperation, trust, courage and love. It has led us to give up on our neighborhoods and turn our backs on neighbors, friends, and extended family, growing increasingly dependent on the government's army of social workers to take care of everything. And now, an observer of our culture takes a close look and accuses us of indifference to the innocent, trusting, family members under our own roofs—our own children.

This is the last period of the game, folks. (You're behind by a zillion points.) Give up on the kids through your conditioned indifference now, and there's no hope for the grandkids. As you sleep, the government is working overtime on all fronts, paving the way to completely take over the responsibilities parents have been taught to forsake. Consider this short list as representative of current activity (but please don't stop here; the activity continues daily; the evidence surrounds you):

• "The Michigan School Health Association... identified *all children in the state as coming from dysfunctional families.* It was suggested that surrogates for children should be found in support groups and that these support groups were best done in school to *minimize parental resistance.*"[3] (Emphasis added.)

• Implementing bigger and better national tests that will soon require national curriculum (in other words, total standardization of conditioning across America).

• Increasing talk about longer school days, longer school years, and starting school at younger and younger ages.

• Using outcome-based education to pull the blanket over our sleeping eyes as the government effectively transforms today's compulsory attendance into a very undemocratic compulsory education. "Outcomes" move beyond academics and include *feelings, attitudes, values, and behavior,* opening the door wide for schools to work in cahoots with social workers who grab the kids who "fail" (meaning resist behavior and attitude control). Therefore, untold numbers of children may be additionally labeled and "require" psychological and emotional invasion of their persons and families.

• Big business wishes to certify children for work based on businesses' own specifications for the product they wish schools to mass produce (that's your children, folks!).

• Big money dumped into social service programs like Head Start (whose benefits fade out by second grade and whose co-creator, Edward Zigler of Yale, proclaims half the programs "useless")[4] and Parents as Teachers, where a friendly representative of the government will show you, sometimes while your child is still *in utero*, their scripted way to parent.

• The infamous United Nations Convention on the Rights of the Child, which sounds great in theory, but removes parental authority and guidance to autonomous children (registration at birth required) whose "rights" are then "guarded" by government workers who may step in any time they determine intervention in the family is necessary.

These are not the actions of institutions concerned with allowing you to make your family life top priority, or to make the US of A a kinder, gentler place for your family. They are intended to take your learned indifference to a final peak: You will willingly, gladly, obediently turn total responsibility for your children over to the will of the state. (They may, however, let you continue changing diapers.)

The research proving that the above methods, more appropriate to totalitarianism than to a republic, better suited to crowd control than to education, don't work today and won't work tomorrow, is out there, ignored daily by a government whose true interests don't include family or real education. The resource section contains books and information *you must check out for yourself.* Nobody is going to knock on your door and read them to you!

"Most people don't give a rat's patootie."
    —Virginia senatorial candidate Oliver North challenging assertions
    that his role in the Iran-contra scandal makes him unfit for office[5]

If the game of life we learned in school is as senseless as it appears, if its intent is a prosperous economy and government instead of thriving individuals, if it is as harmful as our exploration indicates, if it is a game society isn't winning, isn't it time to change the rules? Better yet, isn't it time to accept that our participation in the game keeps it alive, and choose to walk away?

The question is no longer "*can* I teach my own children?" but "can my children and family be truly healthy and happy, functional, free, and educated *if I don't?*" There is a better, different way. It's time to go home—for better answers, for safer communities, for kinder selves. For our children. It's time for examining our priorities.

> Although we can hardly be proud of ourselves for what we are teaching [our children], we should at least be proud of them for how well they've learned our lessons.
> —Benjamin Barber, "America Skips School,"
> *Harper's*, November, 1993

Priorities. Are they children, spouse, home, neighbor, community? Or are they money, job, investments, dealing with stress (physical health-related, as in ulcers and heart attacks; emotional health-related, as in troubles with relationships; or stress over your stress), and/or living up to the American Dream of success no matter the price?

How did your priorities grow? With liberal use of material presented in an insightful, 1989 *Harper's* article by Nicholas Lemann called "Naperville: Stressed Out in Suburbia[6]," here's a micro-tour through very recent modern history. It addresses only one socioeconomic group in the 50's and the late 80's, that of middle class suburbia. While the past and present conditions of dozens of other socioeconomic groups went through different changes in different directions, the main point is that *change has occurred* 1) as dramatically as the change in technology during the same period, 2) in a large percentage of the population and 3) a percentage that was well-observed by fiction and non-fiction writers alike.

Our 50's "model" town is Park Forest, IL. Naperville, IL represents the 1989 version of suburbia.

• A one-story, simple yet highly acceptable Park Forest house sold for $13,000; in Naperville the "flamboyantly traditional" houses sport two stories, ostentatious architectural extras, and will set you back an average $160,000, but could run higher than $500,000.

• Consumer culture was a mere baby back in the 50's. Park Forest residents couldn't hold a candle to their 80's counterparts when it comes to spending.

• While a Park Forest weekday found most mothers home, in Naperville "a ranch-style tract house, a Chevrolet, and meat loaf for dinner will not do any more..."

• Ah, the kids. 50's parents didn't really worry about the kids who played obliviously in the yard while adult life unfolded inside. The Naperville family worries about every step in Junior's development while complaining "between working long hours, traveling on business, and trying to stay in shape they have no free time." (Has worry about the kids replaced raising the kids?)

• Park Forest kids ran home and ate lunch with Mom. Naperville kids eat in the cafeteria, take the bus to after school "care," and stay up too late "visiting" during the only available time with their parents. Naperville parents and school administrators, by the way, complain about school's competitiveness, but alas, the adults are quite competitive, too.

• Neighborhood ties grew through Park Forest-style *kaffeeklatsches*, cocktail and dinner parties, teas, and such. It's no muss-no fuss restaurant fun for Naperville entertainers.

Have you found it, the major change whose waves spread through family, community and culture, transforming our parents' priorities (children, "sufficient" house, time to serve community, time to share with neighbors) into today's priorities?

The spark of consumer culture traveled through our society—including schools—and ignited a blaze, catching fire to every household in America. The change occurred as rapidly as one would expect in the Information Age, but our attention is so focused on the Age's economic and technological aspects, we're too busy to pay much attention to its impact on the individual home.

This is exactly what I'm asking you to do for your family now. Separate your priorities from those of your environment. Think about the evolution of your current priorities. If you could live a life that reflects everything you value, would your priority list change from what it is now? Most likely you already hit upon many clues to this mystery as you met your makers, and you'll put all this information to work (taking it to the Application level of the Education Pyramid) when we get to "Creating Your Family's Personal Education Philosophy."

But for now we're focusing on priorities (as in what's important to you, what always comes first in your life, as in "precedence, especially established by order of importance or urgency").[7]

My guess is you'll find an inordinate amount of time devoted to gathering money. Include the 40—80 hours each week of time actually spent at work, but don't forget time commuting, additional phone calls or paper work from home, evening meetings, time spent shopping for work clothes (and keep in mind for later, shopping for school clothes and materials), time spent preparing meals your family won't enjoy together, any additional time spent on activities that occur on account of your current priorities, and time spent *thinking* about or *unwinding from* stress or discomfort related to gathering money.

While you're at it, figure out time your child devotes to his job, school. Start with the school hours, add get-ready time, travel time, average homework time, school-related-after-school activities, any time you or your child devotes to volunteering, organization meetings, board meetings, etc. Add in any and all time used toward school and related activities. If you really want a clear picture of how little time remains for spending together as a family, add in time spent sleeping, watching TV, and eating, and subtract all from twenty-four hours.

Both work and school follow a common folk law of money and time: Living expenses expand to fill any size income, and school expands to fill family life. And here's the rub: A family's life can be knocked for a loop in direct correlation to its dependence on external providers, like government for education, a corporation for job, insurance and/or pension, peers for identity/love/inclusion, social services for income, aid, or training as a parent... you get the idea. The conclusion is learned dependence controls your family and you to the degree you remain conditioned, to whatever degree you remain asleep.

You can also examine priorities related to the family as they are reflected by the society around you:

• Homelessness—"Americans must look to other sources [besides government] for the moral and spiritual purpose that alone creates and sustains homes."[8]

• Illiteracy—"The illiteracy of the young turns out to be our own reflected back to us with embarrassing force."[9]

• Teen pregnancy/sexual abuse/drug use/gangs/suicide— "Moving out comes easier for adolescents who have not sensed that the house they are leaving behind is their home."[10]

• Marriage—"Marriages with two or three children are less likely to fail than marriages with no children or with only one child."[11]

If examining your priorities uncovers anything you'd like to change, first you need to discover within your Self if you are willing to pay the price. One thing's for sure, the cup must be empty before it can be filled. The "Self-Examining Priorities" pages ahead are included to help you get started.

Researchers put it this way: "Human beings are capable of nuanced decision making when they are not paralyzed by authoritarian hierarchies, conflicting cues, or impersonal structures that diffuse individual responsibility, or when they are involved in decision-making processes that involve *constructing* preferences rather than merely registering them."[12] Throughout this book I put it another way: Gotta let go of that conditioning! Trust yourself to do this and then follow through. You'll find it leads to freedom you can't even imagine right now. I can't describe it to you. You must experience freedom from conditioning—and its inherent benefits—for yourself.

The bad news is there's a gaping chasm between knowing that something is so and acting upon this knowledge, completely and unequivocally integrating it into daily life. The greatest choice a parent has today is not this nonsense about choosing between public schools A, B, and C (a rock, a hard place, and hell), but choosing to *use and act upon* any knowledge you realize leads to real improvement in your child's life.

The good news is that as confusion—and the feeling that there is nothing else out there to grab on to—gives way to experience and, therefore, understanding, the reordering of priorities gets easier and easier and provides satisfaction beyond anything money can buy. New-found hours with the kids turn out to be more real, more significant, than chasing dollars all day. Sharing your Self and keeping your priorities straight in a civilization which is slowly but surely destroying itself, is a more valuable gift to your child than anything you can pick up off a store shelf.

It's also harder to go back to sleep and snuggle into the bliss of ignorance once you wake up. It's got to be comparable to the relief a butterfly feels when she sheds her cocoon and stretches her wings to dry in the noonday sun. A happy family living by its personal priorities is the truest expression of "the right answer." If you allow it, examining your priorities can transform you, like a butterfly, into that graceful expression of parent which was just sleeping inside you all along.

SELF-EXAMINING PRIORITIES

In true family centered education fashion, this is NOT a test. It's meant to serve as a guide in examining your priorities. I'm not going to make this easy for you; there are no right or wrong answers. But when completed, your assessment will provide physical evidence of the more esoteric aspects of your priorities as well as your ability to restructure them.

Take your time, both in answering and reviewing the results. If you uncover aspects of yourself that might stand in the way of reclaiming your family, honestly evaluate your ability to change. You may not be able to teach an old dog new tricks, but humans are remarkably flexible and courageous, particularly when the happiness and contentment of their children are at stake.

Average Day

Time spent at work and work-related activities _____ hours

Child's time spent at school, school-related activities _____ hours

Regarding Time

Always	Sometimes	Never	
____	____	____	Current obligations fill 12 or more hours of my day.
____	____	____	I could drop all of my obligations beyond family and never miss them.
____	____	____	I can organize my time to accomplish things that need to get done.
____	____	____	I'd rather do something myself than watch my child do it slowly or wrong.
____	____	____	I have less time with my family than I did 5/10 years ago.
____	____	____	I spend more time working to make the same amount of money I did 5/10 years ago.
____	____	____	Our family spends equal time on outer world and spiritual matters.
____	____	____	I spend at least an hour a day attending solely to the kids.

Regarding Money

Always	Sometimes	Never	
____	____	____	I'm happy with my economic status quo.
____	____	____	There's never enough money at the end of the month.
____	____	____	Thoreau's ideas about simplicity intrigue me.
____	____	____	It's important that my family have access to modern conveniences.
____	____	____	I spend time at home handling financial matters.
____	____	____	If I see something I want in an ad or on TV, I get it as soon as I can.
____	____	____	Time is money.
____	____	____	I owe too much money.
____	____	____	My lifestyle depends on credit.
____	____	____	I think "poor" people don't work hard enough.
____	____	____	I would move and change my family's life for a job making more money.

Regarding Children

Always	Sometimes	Never	
____	____	____	I like my environment quiet.
____	____	____	I like a lot of activity around me.
____	____	____	I enjoy playing with my children.
____	____	____	I enjoy talking with my children.
____	____	____	I feel there is something missing in my children's lives.
____	____	____	I think my children have a lot of good ideas.
____	____	____	I want my house neat and tidy.
____	____	____	I'm the only one who can clean my home properly.
____	____	____	My house rules are flexible.
____	____	____	I feel I know my children well.
____	____	____	I say I'm sorry to my children when I've made a mistake.
____	____	____	Other children enjoy coming to my home.
____	____	____	I think children can always use a little more attention and hugs.

Always	Sometimes	Never	
____	____	____	If my children came home an hour late and told me their ride was late, I'd believe them.
____	____	____	Peer association is more important than parental guidance.
____	____	____	My children have time to add volunteer work in their lives.
____	____	____	I'd like my children to experience an apprenticeship.
____	____	____	My children pick up habits and behavior I don't like from their friends.
____	____	____	My children pick up habits and behavior I enjoy from their friends.

Regarding School

Always	Sometimes	Never	
____	____	____	I think my tax money is well spent in my local schools.
____	____	____	The results of my children's learning experiences are a reflection of me and my values.
____	____	____	My children are well-balanced physically, mentally, and spiritually as a result of school attendance.
____	____	____	I handle everyday math with confidence.
____	____	____	I can write a letter properly spelled and punctuated.
____	____	____	I worry about my children when they are at school.
____	____	____	We've missed important events because of school schedules.
____	____	____	I see my children applying what they learn in school in their daily lives.
____	____	____	My children's happiness in school is contingent upon that year's teacher.
____	____	____	My children return home from school free of stress.
____	____	____	My children have meaningful relationships in the community outside of school.
____	____	____	I was happy the first day my child left for school.
____	____	____	I recognize incidents of indoctrination when I review my child's school books or papers.
____	____	____	My child's description of school happenings sounds just like when I was in her grade.

Always   Sometimes   Never

_____   _____   _____   I feel comfortable taking my child out of school when necessary.

Regarding Self

Always   Sometimes   Never

_____   _____   _____   What others think is important to me.

_____   _____   _____   I do things differently than my neighbors and friends.

_____   _____   _____   When someone criticizes me, I consider what he said.

_____   _____   _____   I've written to the editor of my local paper.

_____   _____   _____   I tend to form judgments quickly.

_____   _____   _____   I read a lot.

_____   _____   _____   I think a lot.

_____   _____   _____   I enjoy learning new things.

_____   _____   _____   I like knowing what everyone else is doing.

_____   _____   _____   I don't care what everyone else is doing.

_____   _____   _____   My work life is satisfying.

_____   _____   _____   When I find I don't have something I need, I can improvise.

_____   _____   _____   Mistakes mean I'm stupid and clumsy.

_____   _____   _____   Mistakes are learning opportunities.

_____   _____   _____   When I have trouble accomplishing something, I find a different way to proceed.

_____   _____   _____   I'd rather play in a baseball game than watch one.

_____   _____   _____   I care more about whether something works than how it works.

_____   _____   _____   I enjoy finding unique solutions to challenges.

_____   _____   _____   I can pull information together into a coherent report if necessary.

_____   _____   _____   I consider myself a success.

_____   _____   _____   When I invest my time in something, I want results quickly.

_____   _____   _____   I know who I am.

_____   _____   _____   I'm the most self-sufficient person I know.

CHAPTER EIGHT

CREATING YOUR FAMILY'S PERSONAL EDUCATION PHILOSOPHY

And fathers and mothers have lost the idea that the highest aspiration they might have for their children is for them to be wise—as priests, prophets, or philosophers are wise.

—Allan Bloom
in *The Closing of the American Mind*

W hat is *your* family's personal education philosophy? Chances are, like many families fast asleep, you haven't thought deeper than your child receiving a high school diploma and entering the best college you can afford. But since you've gotten this far in this book, I picture you stretching, sensing there *can* be more, even if at this point you haven't quite figured out what it is.

This chapter will help you sort things out by guiding you in preparation of a personal education philosophy (PEP) for your family. It's intended to help you think beyond a diploma, to examine those aspects of Life most important for the children you love. It's important that this philosophy truly be yours, void of external influences and programming that might cloud your thinking. Life is education, education is art, and your family's canvas should reflect your shape, glow with your colors, express your feelings.

You may want your children's learning experience to bestow happiness, fulfillment, a sense of responsibility, self-esteem, and yes, even love in their lives. Perhaps you've recognized the evolutionary changes in mankind and society, and seek to change with them instead of ineffectively trying to hold back the tide any longer. Or maybe you're one of the millions of adults that "see that their own schooling in a large part frustrated, impoverished, and didn't teach us how to think."[1] Any and all of these "reasons" can be woven into the fabric of your education philosophy. Any and all of them can replace school at center stage in your family's life.

I know you're busy. I know your time splits in a dozen different directions each day. And formulating your education philosophy takes much time, as well as deep thought. Please don't look at it as just one more thing to squeeze into your day. It might help you to consider this time and thought an investment in your children's future, for a well-formulated education philosophy will serve many purposes.

• A PEP will help your family clarify its objectives. With a clear understanding of what you and your children want, you can better examine each option available to you.

- A PEP will serve as a map as you begin clearing the foot path your family will follow toward your chosen destination.

- A PEP will help you communicate your decisions to those who might require explanations. This includes but is not limited to your local school administrators and/or school board, pediatrician, any social workers with whom you may be in contact, curious neighbors, skeptical relatives, or the press (this happens to a lot of us!)

- A PEP will keep the "big picture" in front of you. This will aid you in everything from choosing materials that fit your philosophy (saving you money and time) to keeping your perspective when you hit those inevitable "rough spots" along your journey. Today's problems somehow don't seem so bad when you realize it's only one step, and not the entire journey, that's going awry.

- A PEP will increase your confidence in your decisions, your children, and *yourself.*

Just as you wouldn't wander off into the woods without a map or warm, comfortable shoes, there's a few basics you'll want to take with you as you explore your PEP for your comfort and peace of mind. Comfortable shoes aren't a "rule" for being in the woods, but wearing them sure beats getting blisters and snake bites. So, too, the following bits of advice from an ol' camper aren't intended as the last word on PEP preparation. They're meant as a guide, keeping you stepping straight and tall as you proceed.

Step 1: Take Out the Garbage

Have you ever tried to work in a cluttered room, office, or garage only to find that your task moves along twice as quickly after you put useful things where you can find them and throw away the rest?

You can do the same thing for your thinking before you begin formulating your PEP. Now's the time to throw away (forget) everything you think you know about school and learning. Remember, what masquerades as learning in the school institution is a far cry from the real meaning of education. So many of us have school and education twisted and knotted and confused in our memories, it's a huge task to separate the good from the bad, the useful from the garbage. Better to dump the biggest gnarled messes in the trash and start fresh.

You begin by examining each current concept you have about learning under a mental microscope. For example, the thought that you hate math pops into mind. You turn this concept over and over, examining why you think you hate math, when you started thinking you hate math, how this hate affects how you use (or avoid) math today, and so on.

Your observations will shed light on how your feelings evolved, and maybe point out misconceptions or misperceptions you have about math. Let's say you discover that your distaste for the subject surfaced in Mr. Boyer's sixth grade class. You remember you didn't like Mr. Boyer. Mmm, that was also the year the class bully made getting up for school each day sheer misery. Come to think of it, that year there was no basketball because you had to stay after school for help in... math!

Beginning to see how gnarled your ideas really are? Math does not stand alone, but is tangled among, of all things, sixth grade emotions! You realize you've grown emotionally since then, and the feelings you had—hate for a particular teacher and fear of the bully—seem laughable. Math, it appears, wasn't the problem at all!

You've got a million of these knots cluttering your ideas about education, all piled in a messy heap concealing your real thoughts and cloaking the truth. Take your time. Sort through the mess. Save what is right. Ditch what is wrong. It's a dirty (but interesting) job, and only you can do it.

Step 2: Memories

The older we get, the better a backward look on childhood becomes. The more distant childhood becomes, the more school memories resemble professional photographs of pretty girls—fuzzy and "touched up."

You remember the prom, the football games you won, the chemistry class fire, lunch time, and graduation, moments we choose to store in our memories because they were fleeting, beyond the routine of day to day life.

But there were other moments, too, of which Barbra Streisand sang: "What's too painful to remember, we simply choose to forget." I guarantee you've forgotten a lot more about your own education than you remember. But if you are going to make responsible decisions about where and how your child learns, the best experience to guide you is your own. You need to take a good, hard look at your own schooling to provide you with a point of reference, something to which you may compare other educational options and evaluate their relative merit.

We've already touched on the difference between receiving an education and being conditioned or programmed. Now is a good time to apply this knowledge to your own experience. Did each progressive school year leave you feeling more and more capable and in control of your own destiny? As your knowledge base about a particular subject expanded, were you awed by the vast expanse of information that still lay over the horizon? Were you eager each morning to get to class and continue a lesson or project from the day before? Did you feel purpose and see each class' relevance to your future? Do you feel you are a better person for the time you spent in school? Did you feel funny about jumping up and moving at the sound of a bell? Or about moving along crowded hallways like one in a massive herd of cattle?

The paragraph above contains enough food for thought to keep you chewing for a month! Yet there are still more questions around the bend, many more angles from which to get to the heart of the truth about learning and conditioning. Once you get going, they will come to you. Have faith in yourself, and remember it's for the kids.

Here are a few more angles from which to bring up those memories. Start with whichever one you feel most comfortable. There's no magic order to the questions. There aren't any magic answers, either. No one else has had exactly the same school experiences as you have.

- Did school prepare you for life—or work?

- What was good about your school experience? Why?

- What about your experience could have been improved? Why? How? By whom?

- How much of what you learned in school do you apply today?

- How much of what you do today did you learn outside of school?

How can children bombarded from birth by noise, frenetic schedules, and the helter-skelter caretaking of a fast-paced adult world learn to analyze, reflect, ponder? How can they use quiet inner conversations to build personal realities, sharpen and extend their visual reasoning? These qualities are embedded in brains by the experiences a society chooses for its children.
    What are we choosing for ours?
                        —Jane M. Healy, Ph.D. in *Endangered Minds: Why Children Don't Think and What We Can Do About It*

If you discover your "Memories" are more bitter than sweet, don't worry; simply let them go. But keep what remains as a result of your experience (knowledge) to carry you to decisions benefiting the children you love. That which you choose for your children today will become their "Memories" tomorrow. Is it not best, then, to choose with as much knowledge as you have love in your heart?

Step 3: Talk and Read (The Importance of Many Points of View)

I once ran across a definition of a grade (as in grades in school) that appeared in an article titled "Facts and Fancy in Assigning Grades."

"A grade," states the writer, "can be regarded only as an inadequate report of an inaccurate judgment by a biased and variable judge of the extent to which a student has attained an undefined level of mastery of an unknown proportion of an indefinite amount of material."[2] Whew.

Have you ever defined a grade like that? Me neither. Fact is, if you ask a dozen people for a definition, you'll get twelve different ones. It's the same way with opinions, ideas, and recommendations. Not only do we all have a unique perspective on the world, we formulate ideas and make recommendations based on what works for us. There is, of course, no guarantee that someone else will find our ideas and recommendations work as well for them.

Nowhere have I seen this sweetly human phenomenon put through its paces quite the way it is in family centered education. Because it is the closest thing to a grass roots movement education may ever see, because families select it as their option of choice for very personal reasons, and because those reasons are as unique as the families themselves, no one person or organization can possibly speak or write on behalf of all family centered learners (this is not to say that some don't try!).

Expose yourself to lots of different points of view. The first TV news coverage you see about family centered learning may contain footage of kids sitting around the kitchen table reading textbooks. The next thing you discover may be a newsletter produced by a conservative fundamentalist Christian group. The book you pick up in the library may talk about "unschooling" and detail family life free of worksheets, tests, drugs, and peer pressure.

Where one approach might turn you off, another will tickle your imagination. Where one way looks impossible, another might fit very nicely into your family's lifestyle (OK, with a few minor adjustments).

TV, newsletters, and books can introduce you to many different approaches to family centered learning, but nothing beats talking directly with folks who spend every day learning with their children. They can fill you in on all the little details, answer questions you think are silly, and share their stories, helping you realize that even the most successful families started with the same doubts, confusion, and yes, even fear, that you are facing now.

Through trial and error you'll discover a person or group with whom you feel comfortable, and find that these are the people next door or down the street, "normal" folks. They don't have the corner on the patience market which many non-family centered learners suspect. Nor do they possess super-human intelligence, great sums of money, or necessarily radical political views. They *do* possess varied, superbly informed points of view, possibly saving you lots of worry, time, and money.

Talking and reading are perfect supplements to the internal search you are conducting with steps 1 and 2. The many viewpoints you'll encounter will spark new questions and insights, leading you deeper in your self-study, and get you ready for...

Step 4: Putting It Down in Black and White

By now you've spent lots of time reading, talking, thinking, thinking, and thinking. (Your kids are going to love you for it!) It's time to record your personal education philosophy (PEP).

Turn off the TV. Grab your spouse/partner. Bring a stack of paper, a pencil, and a cup of your favorite beverage to your favorite chair. Take a couple of deep breaths. Let your imagination fly.

This is *your* PEP. It's free of "traditional" restraints on what's possible (get rid of those "have tos" and "shoulds!"). It reflects your inspiration, the ideal learning situation for *your* children. Don't censor yourself as you write; put down all notions, even if they are still in abstract form. Even if, at first glance, they seem silly or impossible.

Chances are you'll start off with some very broad goals, as in "I want my child to be a compassionate, caring adult." Write that down. Brainstorm a little: What activities could he engage in that will bring out compassion? (Examples: Spend time helping an elderly neighbor, learn about Somalia/Sarajevo/holocaust, etc., contact local Red Cross and find out what they do, volunteer at the animal shelter...) What family situation would allow your child to accomplish this? (Mom and Dad at work all day? Mom home? Dad home? Can he walk or does he need rides?...) What educational situation would allow time for this? (Public school? Alternative school? At home? Religious school?...) What can you do to help this come about? (Watch the news together, have daily family discussions, go to the animal shelter with him, visit the library and read biographies of "helpers"...)

Get the kids involved. Talk. Listen. Include their personal interests even if, at this point, these are only collecting baseball cards and playing guitar. These may seem trivial, but could very well become the gates through which your children reach the Application and Connection levels of the Education Pyramid.

> She had seen me interviewed so many times on TV, perhaps she thought that was the only way she could find out the truth. Watching her, I felt guilty about the degree to which my career— and my illness—have robbed me of crucial time with my children.
> —Lee Atwater (former Bush campaign manager)

Maybe you have a more specific educational goal from which to start, such as a good understanding of earth sciences toward an ecologically healthy lifestyle. Write it down. Ask the same questions as above. Think. Record your answers. (If visiting a Brazilian rain forest crosses your mind, write it down. Sure it sounds impossible, but that thought can lead you to a dozen other activities you *can* do.) Ask a few more questions of your own. Get excited. Imagine countless possibilities.

Don't count on accomplishing this in one sitting. Leave your brainstorming papers somewhere handy so you can jot down ideas as they occur. Take a week. Take a month. Take as long as you need to feel you've covered all the aspects of learning you and your children consider important.

Congrats—you're almost done. Hang in there. It's time to get organized. Gather the important, basic goals together in a list or in another form that proves useful to you. Answers to your questions can be inspected from two points of view; 1) how "doable" is it under your present circumstances and 2) how "doable" is it if, in fact, your family's priorities will change, creating time and freedom to pursue this? See the sample at the end of this chapter for some visual stimulation and ideas.

Take another sheet of paper and list just a few of the activities that achieve each goal, make a column for each of the educational approaches, and place a check mark under the ones that are realistic paths to accomplishment. (For example, I wouldn't take a Chevy to the moon, and I wouldn't take public school as a route to nourishing compassion in my children.) Maybe you'd like to make a similar chart with columns for the family situations you considered earlier. Be creative. Formulate your information in any style that serves your needs, clarifies your thinking, and makes it easiest for you to use what you have created.

At this point the handwriting is all but on the wall. It's time to...

Step 5: Use Your PEP As a Guide In Decision Making

If your PEP is thorough, clearly written, and reflects your true aspirations free of conditioning and self-doubt, this will be the easiest step of all! The initial decision of "where do we go from here?" is staring you right in the face. All you need to do is say "yes" to the best alternative, or realize that you must settle for second, or third, or fourth best, or combine two or three alternatives to cover all your bases. (Note: Some states allow family centered educators to pick and choose a healthy balance, combining school attendance for particular subjects with learning at home. Other states, however, only give lip service to having your child's best educational interests at heart, and force you to make an all-or-nothing decision. Check with a local support group to find the situation in your own state.)

Whatever your decision, you now possess a useful tool you and your children can consult anytime for inspiration, guidance, or a reminder of the "big picture" when your educational approach requires some adjustment.

If your PEP leads you to family centered learning, you have a wonderful head start on preparing any paperwork your state deems necessary. You have direction in your search for materials and/or curriculum you may want. You have a ready-made list of terrific activities; you and your children can plunge right in!

Your PEP can be a future tool, too. If today you must settle for other than your first educational choice, who knows what changes tomorrow may bring? A promotion, a move, a job shift, or a new home business are just a few circumstances that could alter your lifestyle, thus giving you a new perspective from which to analyze your PEP.

Preparing your PEP is a liberating experience, an exercise in freedom to see yourself as you really are and to use this knowledge improving your family's quality of life. You very well may be the first person on your block to create a PEP, for it is not a traditional exercise. But tradition should, at the very least, be open to inspection.

No matter what your findings they are yours and yours alone. Use them well.

SAMPLES FOR YOUR PEP *(with love for all who may learn best visually)*

Basic Goal	Under Current Circumstances	With Priority Changes	Worth Doing
• Jason to pursue, in more depth, his 5-year interest in music and composition	√		√
• For the kids to learn through travel		√	√
• Beth to have more time working/researching with the naturalists at the Nature Center		√	√
• I would like more time with Bob to strengthen values I don't see reflected in his life		√	√
• Andrea wants to raise exotic birds		√	√
• Rachel hates reading. Is important she discover it's a wonderful tool		√	√

Basic Goal "Doable" in:	Public School	Private	At Home	Religious
• Jason to pursue, in more depth, his 5-year interest in music and composition		√	√	
• For the kids to learn through travel			√	
• Beth to have more time working/researching with the naturalists at the Nature Center		√	√	
• I would like more time with Bob to strengthen values I don't see reflected in his life			√	√
• Andrea wants to raise exotic birds			√	
• Rachel hates reading. Is important she discover it's a wonderful tool.		√	√	

CHAPTER NINE

EXPLODING THE TOP FIVE MYTHS ABOUT
FAMILY CENTERED LEARNING
(OR HOMESCHOOLING)

The child is not the mere creature of the state; those who
nurture him and direct his destiny have the right, coupled
with the high duty, to recognize and prepare him for additional obligations.

—U.S. Supreme Court 268 U.S. 510 (1925)

Y ou've probably noticed by now I ask a lot of questions. And I ask you to ask yourself even more. It's because the solutions to a lot of the problems your family may be experiencing as a result of your conditioning are lying, still and deep, inside you.

Certainly you should question others. They can give you lots of the "technical" information you can use to live according to new priorities.

But when it comes to the basics, the "nitty gritty," others can't help you. Where does the commitment come from? Where does the highly touted "patience" come from? Where do the most essential inner qualities —courage and trust —come from?

They emerge from inside you, the same person who possesses the most important answers to the questions set before you.

We now come to a new level of understanding in our journey. Just as you had to throw away the garbage (what you think you know about school and learning) to explore your own education, it's time to toss out the garbage that may be in your mind regarding family centered education, or homeschooling, as it has been dubbed by media, educators, and practitioners.

There's a lot of information out there on homeschooling now, some good, some bad, some true, some false. Since it is our human nature to form images based on perceptions that may not prove accurate, and all information that we receive is understood only in relation to what has passed before, I'm concerned about some of the existing homeschooling myths. Perceptions you have right now were made, perhaps, before you looked more closely at your own schooling and school in general, and saw that government's way is only one way to go about educating children, and a pitifully poor one at that. There are lots of other ways. Family centered education is the one I know and love and chose for many, many reasons. I see so much potential to bring happiness to even more homes, so much potential for positive change in our communities, I want to shout about it from the rooftops. (Fortunately for my neighbors, this book will have to do!) I hope all parents can re-discover family centered learning in the coming pages, viewing it with eyes fresh from a deep sleep, and hearts and minds open to that "something different" we've all been taught to avoid in our pursuit of the plain ol' familiar and comfortable.

Let's do some myth-exploding, shall we?

> True openness means closedness to all the charms that make us comfortable with the present.
> —Allan Bloom in *The Closing of the American Mind*

Myth #1: Homeschooling is school-at-home.

A lot of "homeschoolers" don't like the term homeschooling because it perpetuates the myth. What else, after all, could something called "homeschooling" be but "school-at-home?!"

I had school at home when our family first started. Many families did, for it was the only thing we knew. But we kept reading, kept talking, kept sharing, kept learning.

We reached a critical point of awareness and asked ourselves, "Is it *really* necessary to turn the gentle art of reading into 9,788 components for eight years' worth of workbooks?" The answer unfolded before us. Apparently not, for youngsters who spend each day discussing all manner of books read on the couch, write and illustrate stories and letters that Mom transcribes, and fall asleep imagining what will happen next in *Little House on the Prairie* seem to pick up reading skills with a small dose of simple, loving guidance accompanied by a large dose of internal motivation. And guess what? They have been heard saying "I *like* reading!" Homeschooled kids have been spotted throughout the country leaving community libraries with *bags* full of books *they want to read...*

Mmm, if there's no need to do school-at-home with reading, maybe there's another way to approach science? Math? Art? History? And we learned, at the differing rates at which we woke up, exercised our new-found freedom, found trust in ourselves and our kids, risked experiment and failure and returned to the drawing board, that there were, indeed, many, many interesting and exciting ways to go about the business of learning.

We also discover the more we relax, the more learning unfolds as a natural expression of being alive. Our kids are, in fact, "growing without schooling."[1]

We're free to do things you can't do in school. We can make noise; we can talk to each other; we can help each other; we can take as long as we want when a topic or book captures our interest; we can follow our hearts and interests wherever they lead; we can make mistakes without ridicule and attempt something new without fear of being graded, judged, and labeled should we reach a bit too high. We can do many of those things research shows increase the odds of children enjoying the learning experience. We can practice the art of education.

Growing evidence suggests that learning in a natural environment (at least for rats) actually increases the size of the brain cortex, and lets neurons develop more dendrite spines and, probably, more synapses (the points at which nerve impulses pass from one neuron's axon to another's dendrite). Though "the mere existence of many synapses does not necessarily mean 'smarter,' this potential for change is indeed impressive."

The details aren't as important here as the promise of results so we'll get right to the laboratory and the rat experiment. All rats get equal food and water, but an "enriched" group gets a bigger cage, more friends, and lots of toys to explore. As you might expect, the enriched groups' brains had "differences in synapses as great as 20-25% in one area of the cortex." This is as far as the knowledge gained from this type of study usually goes, but listen to this:

"Even the 'enriched' environments are less stimulating than those in nature where rats are constantly exposed to the real challenges of living in a free environment, finding food, defending themselves, and moving about when and where they wish. Animals growing up 'in the wild' ...outside...[the] laboratory tend to have larger and heavier cortexes than do those raised in the cages." This includes the "enriched" cages, which you might look at as "good" rat schools. And another tidbit should help you trust nature and your child: "Brains —and the organisms attached to them —tend to gravitate to the types of stimulation that they need at different stages of development."[2]

The reality of school-at-home does exist in some homes, and it remains an individual family's choice how far they will stretch their wings or how far they will trust the natural tendency of a child to learn what he needs at a particular time and place. The point is you don't have to have anybody's school-at-home if that's not how you want to spend your days. Don't let the thought of having to remodel your home to resemble the classrooms of your memory deter you from further consideration of family centered education. You can get rid of the desks and chalkboards and grade book and worksheets. More importantly, you can move beyond the behavior management, classroom discipline, and the conditioning for robotic citizenship toward guiding young people to personal and community fulfillment. Family centered learning is an education option that can truly be whatever you have the trust and courage to make it.

Myth #2: Homeschooling takes place in isolation at home.

When researchers got around to studying homeschooled children (that darn "education phenomenon" just won't go away!) they proved on paper what home educators already knew in their hearts —homeschooling works. There now exist enough studies to quiet even the most skeptical observer with incontrovertible evidence.

So what's a giant education institution to do; close its text books, send millions of administrators and teachers home, apologize to the American public for their hundred-plus year scam, and make restitution for the $1 billion spent on education *every day?* [3]

Yeah. Right.

The establishment settled for criticism of homeschoolers' socialization, or their perceived lack thereof. (The reality of homeschoolers scoring better than their traditionally schooled counterparts on the Piers-Harris Self Concept Scale which measures such things, as well as subsequent research by University of Florida College of Education doctoral student Larry Shyers showing homeschooled kids behaving "better" in a room with schooled kids doesn't fit into the logic here, but let's keep going, anyway.)

The education institution, in the form of individual teachers and administrators, teachers unions and national organizations, continues to perpetuate this myth each time it is contacted for its side of media stories on home education.

The truth is when we look at the real meaning of education, *public school* is an isolating experience. Stuck within the restraints of four walls, scrutinized by authoritative figures every moment, surrounded only by same-age peers likewise confined in an artificially created society, and having every day planned down to the minute by someone else, children in public school are isolated from the one place real learning effectively occurs —the real world.

Sure, family centered learners spend a lot of time at home; there's a lot to do! If people are looking at this time through their own conditioning, they probably don't understand that these children fill their days with activities and topics that propel them to the next activity and topic. The critic may see isolation, but any discussion of homeschooling isolation (or socialization) is moot if we remember one important fact about children. They have a wonderful ability to accept as "normal" whatever circumstance exists. A child who has never seen GI Joe or Barbie's Dream House *doesn't* desire to own one. Nor does a child who hasn't been surrounded by numerous other children feel as if he is missing something. Conflict arises only in the mind of the adult who feels that circumstances should be different.[4]

> Whenever I had second thoughts about the socialization my children may have been missing by homeschooling, I'd take them to a G-rated matinee movie. One look around the theater at the running, screaming, popcorn-throwing little socialites was enough to overcome my doubts.
> —Mario Pagnoni in *The Complete Home Educator*

Socialization is a concept, a generalized idea emphasized way out of proportion to its value as it exists in schools today. Beyond the fact that the artificiality of being surrounded by and interacting solely with others who are the same age is never repeated in the real world, the "world" of public school happens to be the breeding ground of many families' problems, including alcohol and other drugs, violence, promiscuous sex, competition, and an increasingly negative attitude towards learning in children.

Drawing on their own experience, most adults will tell a youngster who will listen it's not the quantity of friends you have, it's the quality of your relationships, usually nurtured and sustained with a few, select friends. What stops us from seeing this truth when it comes to school? Only the hype —and our lifelong conditioning — to the contrary.

Just in case you're still worried, let me reassure you —the family centered educators I know and read about have, by far, richer, more rewarding social lives than anybody else I know. Homeschool support group families get together for everything from play groups to baseball teams to whale watching to theater productions to camp-outs to roller skating. There's Scouts, 4-H, church choir and Civil Air Patrol. Swim classes, sports teams, lessons in crafts, sign language, martial arts, foreign language, computers, fishing, sewing, woodworking and cooking. Trips to museums, historical sites, planetariums, state capitols, TV stations, nature centers and bagel bakeries. Volunteer work for hospitals, humane societies, fire departments, libraries, soup kitchens, food pantries, nursing homes, museums, political campaigns, science institutes, photographers, veterinarians, computer programmers, churches, artisans and their own home businesses. And more. Much, much more.

All these activities put children in touch with real people (young, old and in-between) doing real work (hard, soft, interesting) in real settings (indoors, outdoors, cooperatively) in the real world (warts and all).

Family centered education expands beyond the walls of home into the neighborhood where children and community members willing to share their knowledge and time enter a rewarding, stimulating win-win relationship.

Maybe we shouldn't tell too many bureaucrats how rich the social lives of homeschoolers really are. They're liable to pull out their microscopes and look for a new angle to criticize! But if the cry of "isolated" gets to you, go ahead and holler "No way!"

Myth #3: Mom needs to be a teacher.

Those of us who started our homeschool journey with school-at-home were usually under the spell of this myth, too. Our conditioning led us to believe we had to don yet another hat and stand at the head of the class pouring forth facts, *acting* as we presumed teachers are supposed to act.

There are two misconceptions rolled into this one myth. The first and most obvious is you have already spent years filling the role of teacher under the label of parent. With every interaction with your child during her first five years of life you teach her with your words, your actions, your examples. With your guidance she learned how to walk, talk, throw and catch a ball, ride a bike, drink from a cup, kiss good-night. These feats didn't require a different hat; they required your commitment, your love, and your trust that *when she was ready* your child would accomplish all of these and more. Consider just one of these accomplishments. Let's take the incredibly complex action of talking and making sense of sounds as they become meaningful communication. You didn't have a text book (or accompanying teacher's manual). You didn't break the subject of speech into minute sections and drill her end-lessly on each piece. You simply spoke with her, encouraging her babbling each time you replied and smiled and hugged her.

She listened. She experimented. She happily drooled while rolling and teasing her tongue into new positions until that momentous day she stumbled upon "Dada."

Did you look at her with scorn and say, "The proper way to pro-nounce your father's name is Dad (points off for adding an A at the end) or Daddy (go back and say it fifty times with a Y)?" You, as parent/teacher, giddy with happiness in what she *did* accom-plish, showed her through your love and approval that she was on the right track. Her inner motivation compelled her; your atten-tion guided her. She learned.

The method you use as parent in your child's first five years is nature's way. Your sustained relationship in an atmosphere of safety and trust and acceptance is the essence of education as art. The "information" doesn't come *from* you, it flows *through* you, through your conscious and subconscious messages; the tone of your voice, your face, your body language, your deeds. The "learning" isn't done *to* your baby, it *comes from* her. It's when we go against our nature that mankind gets in trouble. As they are set up now, schools work against nature. You don't have to.

Throw the teacher's hat away. The hat you are already wearing fits you just fine. And it's beautiful.

The second misconception associated with this myth about homeschooling is that even if you choose to follow public school's method, teaching is not as difficult a task as all the college years, certificates, and teachers unions would lead you to conclude it is. Remember, you begin with a more intimate knowledge of your child's likes and dislikes, strengths and weaknesses, needs and personality than any teacher will ever glean about her in a classroom filled with dozens of other children. If you need to choose between three text books, for instance, you have a pretty good idea which one your son would prefer (better yet, you can ask him!). In the classroom, one book must fit all.

If you've never examined materials provided to teachers for classroom use, you'll be surprised, perhaps shocked, at how simplistic their directions are. I once attended a two-day long teachers' seminar sponsored, in part, by a public television station. Its purpose was to help teachers integrate public TV into their day. In each of the eight or so workshops, the trained instructors spent much of the time teaching us how to press a VCR's pause button, showing us where the accompanying paperwork told us exactly where in the program to stop it, and what to say/ask while it was stopped. Choreographed down to the minute, the presentations intended for classroom-use appeared to my non-teacher-trained eyes like a play rehearsal. Here's the script, say this now, ask that then, push the button here (smile and take a bow).

> *In the workshop on presenting the function of skeletal bones to elementary-age children, my group received a box of popsicle sticks from which we were to construct a three-dimensional frame. When that was complete, we connected bones for a paper skeleton with brass fasteners. After class I called home. While I had been sitting inside playing with popsicle sticks, my three "teacherless" children were out in the woods in the fresh air constructing a fort which, within a short period of time, sported a roof, smoke hole, and a second story lookout deck.*

Standardized tests contain the same type of step-by-step directions for administration, easily followed by anyone who can read. Some states require home educators to attend a training class before giving the tests to their children. Before I attended a seminar I couldn't imagine the class needing to last more than five minutes, but now I see how the presenters could fill a couple of hours.

If teachers' lessons are a community playhouse production,

management techniques are full-scale Broadway productions. Browsing through the February, 1994 issue of *Education Digest* (the *Reader's Digest* of the education world), I encountered two enlightening articles about classroom management.

1. "When Parents Get Aggressive," Lorna Brooks-Bonner, from *School Safety:* You (teacher) have to diffuse "angry mama's" hostility, so "a strong, clear, forceful voice demonstrates your concern." "Position your body at an angle —keeping a distance of at least three feet." "Keep your hands open; do not make a fist." "Do not break eye contact." When a school counselor joins in the action "...the counselor and I will play roles of 'good guy vs. bad guy.'"

And you thought *you* went into those parent-teacher meetings prepared?!

2. "Practical Peacemaking for Educators," Peter Martin Commanday: To overcome their "sense of powerlessness in today's classroom," teachers are advised "to formulate...a guide for practical behavior in school each day."

The goal, we're told, "is to win small, sequential victories." I'm taking these excerpts from Concept 3 of the six explained, and the summary.

A student (John) has picked up a chair during words with another student. Get his visual attention with a comment. "Using both hands, not one, with palms up and fingers together, you motion toward the area [where you want the chair]. Be sure that one hand is slightly in front of the other..." "Take a step to the side, on a diagonal..." "No longer can we assume that we will be able to command immediate obedience."

Obviously you won't have to deal with these problems in your home. I share them with you because I know you may believe the myth, and these are just two examples of where today's teachers must, of necessity, focus their training and "professionalism." You can spend your time focused on tasks important to and only related to learning.

I am not saying there are not good teachers out there. The difference between a good and bad teacher is not which script she's using, but whether or not she's also using her heart and her soul. You will naturally use your heart and soul, and you *can* read the script. And if you're fortunate, there will come a day when you throw the script away, work with nature, and enjoy learning as a process, not a show.

This is the art of education.

Myth #4: Homeschooling is only practiced by "earth mommas" and fundamentalist Christians.

Seems like we always pick the extreme portrayals when we want to represent something we don't fully understand, something foreign to our way of thinking, particularly when it comes to different cultures. Stereotypes seem to fill our need for an image to compensate for our lack of understanding.

Homeschooling is an education experience occuring within the 90's American culture, yet the practice can create so much change in a family's outlook and lifestyle, it might well be said it is a culture within a culture.

Many homeschoolers today are Christian fundamentalists. The percentage, just like the actual number of total home educators, is anybody's guess, reflecting only the perspective of the guesser in any case.

The image of earth mommas rises, perhaps, from the practitioners who carry the idealism of the 60's into their adult lives, shunning society's makers for a world in which self-sufficiency, self-determination, and the study of Self reign supreme. Family centered education becomes a natural extension of a lifestyle where children learn through growing food, storing harvests, tending animals, building shelters for family and livestock, and gathering fuel for winter. Successful accomplishment of any one of these activities requires the acquisition of skills that reach across a typical school curriculum and stretch far beyond it into a knowledge of planning, schedules, attention to detail, and organization, all backed by obvious value and meaning in the context of the children's lives.

Family centered education in some cases will be used for ends with which you may or may not agree. The freedom inherent in home education, just like any freedom afforded man, is always subject to individual choice. You can choose to make a career out of showing others the error of their ways, or you can choose to embrace your own freedom and let it carry you and yours to personally chosen heights.

And that's the point in expoding this myth: Homeschooling is practiced by families that defy categorization or stereotype. You don't have to be an earth momma or a fundamentalist Christian. You can be what you truly are!

Today homeschooling parents include doctors, carpenters, lawyers, plumbers, writers, account executives, trash collectors, hotel managers, actresses, salespeople, and (interestingly) many school teachers.

People you may already know something about grew up as homeschoolers in one form or another: Thomas Edison, William F. Buckley, Jr., Agatha Christie, Andrew and Jamie Wyeth, Alexander Graham Bell, John Burroughs, Albert Schweitzer, Winston Churchill, the Wright Brothers, Leonardo da Vinci, Douglas MacArthur, and Presidents John Q. Adams, Harrison, Lincoln, Madison, Franklin D. Roosevelt, Washington, and Wilson. I doubt all these folks had earth mommas or Christian fundamentalists as parents!

As your knowledge of family centered education expands through reading and meeting homeschoolers, you'll find that these mythical images are mostly conveniences for the media, merely representative of an emerging culture far too diverse to be shoved into any currently existing category.

Whether homeschooling families are to the political left or right; practicing Buddhism, Christianity or no organized religion at all; are rich, poor, or on welfare; living in Manhattan or Alaska; residing in a mobile home park, a split-level, or a teepee, they share one distinguishing characteristic —their children's learning experience is based on family values and grounded in the love and respect that blossom when the family heads the priority list.

Myth #5: Homeschooling is undemocratic.

Homeschool fault-finders have had a lot of fun tossing this myth about. The only rationale I can find for this blatant lie is that critics, most likely A-students from government-sponsored universities, consider the status quo democracy. Therefore, any action that bypasses or, in their perspective, threatens the status quo must be undemocratic.

Many critics fondly quote Thomas Jefferson who, after witnessing the horror of the French revolution, renewed his commitment to an informed citizenship. The part of Jefferson's beliefs that critics forget is his commitment to "reason and free inquiry [as] the only effectual agents against error."

To assume, and then further build an argument for 1990's public education on Jefferson's vision of an informed citizenship is, once again, commencing from a wrong starting place. For Jefferson, reason and free inquiry were essential ingredients of education. The lack of these qualities in 20th century public education is painfully evident everywhere from politics to economics to religion to our family lives and everything in between.

Family centered learning provides its students (and teachers) a rare opportunity for free inquiry. Unshackled from dogma, propaganda, watered-down textbooks, conformity, learned dependence, behavior modification and politically correct teachers, every inquiry is free. Free inquiry *must* occur if we are to learn how to freely think. Free thinking *must* occur if we are to be truly educated. True education *must* occur if we hope to ever find our way back to a society capable of free inquiry.

> A good professor is a bastard perverse enough to think what he thinks is important, not what government thinks is important.
> —Edward C. Banfield, Professor of Government, Harvard University

I can't think of any educational approach more undemocratic than public school. From its more innocuous practices —telling you where to sit, stand and take your place in line; what books to read; what days you must show up; when to talk, change rooms, eat, and relieve yourself; to its spirit-destroying teachings —you are in competition with and cannot trust your classmates; you cannot trust your own thoughts so we will give you ours; you must be graded, scrutinized and, if necessary, humiliated; you must respond to reward and punishment; you must enter the acquisition race and shun the spiritual —public schooling is worse than undemocratic. It rapes young minds and murders human spirit. It is society-sanctioned child abuse.

The freedom necessary to inquire and reason is alive and well and growing in America —in family centered educators' homes. The practice does, in fact, by-pass the status quo. If you believe the higher estimates of current practitioners (and factor in home-schooling's phenomenal growth rate), it does, in fact, threaten the status quo. But at the same time it is one of the purest practices of democracy alive today.

It is up to you to decide for yourself if the status quo —a failing national education system that U.S. Secretary of Education Richard Riley questions "whether [it is] changing fast enough to save and educate this generation of young people," —is worth protecting. The price for this protection, we're finding, is your family's very life, liberty, and pursuit of meaningful happiness.

> As the happiness of the people is the sole end of government, so the consent of the people is the only foundation of it.
>
> —John Adams

CHAPTER TEN

IMAGINE
A Day of Family Centered Education

Would that this institution—or some institution—could become the University of Utopia. What will it be like? It will be the most enlightened institution of higher learning in the world today... Its only purpose is to educate. What a radically novel idea for an institution of higher learning!

—Chas. McCurdy, Jr., Executive Secretary
State Universities Association June 1, 1957
at Gustavus Adolphus College

Y our home is a most ideal place to realize Charles McCurdy's vision of a University of Utopia whose "only purpose is to educate." After all, life, glistening with glorious ups and downs, highs and lows, sadness and pure joy, is a natural learning ground where universal life skills can be demonstrated, experimented with and attained.

This "radically novel idea" is unfolding, in varying degrees, in homes across the country. Families step along the path at their own pace, experimenting with freedom in a thousand different ways, fully aware that learning is a never-ending journey that has little to do with institutions and everything to do with life.

If you've got a lot of things to do, take a break from reading until you can come back and quietly read this chapter. If you can grab a few moments, now, all the better. Let's take a much closer, relaxed look at a day of family centered learning that puts you and yours center stage.

Unplug the phone. Settle into your favorite chair, sitting straight, and press against it as if you are trying to push through. Relax. Do it a few more times, inhaling deeply as you tense and press, exhaling fully as you relax. Take a moment and close your eyes, still relaxing with your breath. Let go of stored tension; let go of thoughts; let go of noise. Let go. Open your eyes again when you are relaxed and ready. (If at all possible, have someone read the next section to you, so you can keep your eyes closed and remain optimally relaxed.)

As day's first light creeps in the window, your early bird child grabs a book and finishes the last two chapters. By this time you're ready to greet the day, and you and early bird get breakfast on the table. He squeezes some fresh grapefruit juice, carefully saving the seeds to add to a growing, cataloged collection. The last child wakes up and joins you just as the school bus rumbles past the house.

The day's plan unfolds as all share what they would like to do. Since you are all taking the classes together, you practice your sign language as you communicate. (The kids graciously remind you there's a sign for "reading" so you don't have to spell it out with your fingers!) One child runs to get the sign language book to look up "videotape," and shows everyone the tricky sign for "correspondence" he discovers as he flips through the pages. You sign, "Catching up on correspondence today is a very good idea—I will." Your youngest signs, "Me, too!" After feeding pets, clearing the table and doing the dishes, everyone dresses and pitches in with the chores as the London Symphony Orchestra's performance of Beethoven's Symphony No. 5 in C Minor permeates the house from the living room record player. Your spouse takes out the trash; you straighten out the video tapes and find the "Nova" recording your daughter asked about at breakfast. One child starts the laundry, another sweeps and mops the kitchen floor, and (if you have a third!) he cleans the cat litter and walks the dog up to the garden where he checks how much longer it might be until his favorite radishes grace the salad bowl again. Any day now, he figures, as he pulls a few weeds before returning to the house.

He enters and finds everyone gathered in the living room waiting to read the next chapter of Homer's *Odyssey*. Yesterday you left Ulysses with Athene, finally washed ashore Ithaca after a twenty-year absence, and nobody can wait to find out how he'll rescue his sweet Penelope from the scoundrel suitors who invade his home and threaten his son, Telemachus.

You leave Ulysses perched on the edge of battle until tomorrow, then your daughter settles down to learn more about dolphins from "Nova." Your oldest child jogs down the street to walk and feed a new puppy for neighbors away at work. Before he comes back inside, he checks the acidity of last night's rain water and dutifully records test results and amount of rainfall in the records he's kept for a year now.

A younger child asks for help as he sets up his favorite game from the *Family Math* book. You play a while, realizing that the game has taught him probability and statistics well. He'll soon move on to Cartesian graphs, and you make a mental note to dig out the graph paper you know you have (somewhere!).

When the game is over, you grab paper, envelopes, stamps, and pen, and tackle that correspondence you promised yourself you would. Your child joins in, writing to his pen pal across the country, carefully numbering the answers to the trivia questions the pen

him. Your joint desk, the kitchen table, is soon cov-
cyclopedias and other reference books as he searches
stions to send his friend to answer. ("No, son," you
say, "I don't know who David G. Farragut is. Tell me about him."
You stop writing as you learn all about the first U.S. Navy Admiral
who commanded his own ship at the age of twelve.) "Nova" is
over, so your daughter begins double-checking her brother's trivia answers, but gets lost in a reference book's section on fashion
design.

Hungry bellies tell everyone it's time for lunch. Talk about
David Farragut and 19th century hemlines shifts to tuna fish salad,
and your budding biographer turns into the "world's best tuna
sandwich maker." The other kids heat last night's leftover turkey
soup as they whip up half a batch of their favorite biscuits. (You
can smell them; they're almost done.) You listen to public radio
news as each eats his fill, turning the radio off when a story about
local landfills leads to a discussion of the politics of environmental
management. Your oldest child decides to write a letter to the editor of the local paper urging residents to consider the pros and
cons of a new waste station carefully.

With lunch over, he starts his letter. The "world's best tuna
sandwich maker" wants to stop at the library when you take his
sister to her volunteer work at the Humane Society. He returns last
week's stack of books before heading to the card catalog in search
of books on volcanoes. ("Yes, I guess we *will* need a bag for all
these books, thank you!") Since you are out and about, you decide
to stop at the grocery store.

You check your wallet and tell your son you have $20 to spend.
He pulls out paper and pencil, and the two of you brainstorm the
best way to spend the money based on your collective memories
of where your cupboards are most bare. Your son's entries of ice
cream, Fritos, cupcakes, and Snickers disappear one by one as he
estimates that the milk, eggs, yogurt, bread, potatoes, and bananas
will do in that $20 bill.

After careful inspection, he chooses the healthiest-looking
bananas, then leads you through the store aisles, checking unit
prices of the various brands of the remaining items on your list. A
quick estimation of money spent reveals you can pick up *one* of the
treats previously crossed off. He decides ice cream will please the
most family members at the lowest cost, and figures that the brand

on sale saves the family eighty-five cents. (Doesn't he look proud?)

As he's bagging the groceries, he notices a frail, elderly woman in trouble as she tries to weave an overloaded cart among the empty ones strewn in her path. Your son clears out the maze and offers to take the groceries to the woman's car. She gratefully accepts his offer, and he returns just in time to help you, too.

By the time you arrive back home, your oldest child has repaired the lawn mower (and changed the spark plug and oil) and his letter is ready to go. He grabs the rest of the family's mail, and delivers it all to the post office on his bike. On the return trip, the neighbor pays him for this week's puppy care. Another neighbor, a former Boy Scout who likes sharing his fifty year-old memories and mementos on occasion, waves and inquires about your son's last Scout camping trip and his teaching duties at the Nature Center.

He's home now, inviting his brother's help in setting up Experiment #47 from the family's electronics kit. The youngest leaves his work on a rapidly expanding 18th century Mill Town panorama and joins him. The two work side by side for the rest of the afternoon, promising to clear off the kitchen table before you return from picking up their sister.

You enter the Humane Society and find out your daughter is back in the examining room. (You can smell this, too, can't you?!) You look closely at your little girl's face and see she is focused, concentrating on the task at hand—performing tests for feline leukemia on a litter of kittens who just arrived. You use the extra time to say hello to the facility's manager and discover your daughter spent part of the afternoon answering questions by phone, and greeting and helping potential pet owners who visited that day. After a quick round of the facilities to say good-bye to everyone (pets and people), her job ends for the day.

The shelter is crowded, you learn, and several "favorite" dogs and cats were put to sleep since her last work day. You acknowledge her sadness, and talk about death—and responsibility. You hear new understanding in her words. You feel her awakening. (She is growing beautifully, isn't she?)

Your sons already set the table and picked some fresh lettuce, carrots, and a couple of too tiny but edible cucumbers from the garden, so your daughter makes a salad while you prepare spaghetti. She hasn't gotten everything out of her system regarding people's irresponsibility to animals, so conversation continues until she feels better. Dinner is over.

One son goes next door to play basketball with a friend. The others soon finish a lesson in their math books and ask you to join in a game of "Where in the World?" You hope you can remember half the countries they do, for it's been quite a while since you've won!

You don't win the board game. But you realize your whole family is winning the game of life when, after all the good-nights are said and kissed and hugged away, you see your daughter's light still burning as she works on her fiction story based on a recently discovered, local story of the disappearance of a female college professor in 1933. You know everyone's winning because whatever your children do tomorrow, they will enjoy. Whatever they enjoy, they will carry away and make a part of themselves.

You fall asleep, wondering where Homer's *Odyssey* will next take Ulysses, wondering where your own family's Odyssey will next carry your children.

Wiggle your fingers and toes, then take a nice, long stretch. Were you and your children flowing through a learning day together? Real circumstances will be different depending on the number and ages of your children, as well as your living situation, but that's OK. What's important here is the *feel* of a day free of school schedules and their associated conditioning and stress.

Let's take a moment and review the education that permeated our day. We'll categorize the experiences into a sort of "educationese," placing activities in the slots, or subject areas, from which they are typically viewed by institutionalized eyes.

MATHEMATICS
Probability and statistics
Money Management
—Estimation
—Comparison shopping
    (price per unit)

SOCIAL STUDIES
History - U.S. Navy & David
    Farragut
History of Clothing
Creation of 18th Century Mill Town

Textbook lessons (pre-algebra, decimals/fractions/percentages)

Where in the World? - familiarity with location of world's countries

Local history - 1933

LANGUAGE ARTS

Classic Literature and fiction reading

Friendly letter writing—punctuation, grammar, spelling, sentence & paragraph structure, effective communication

Business letter writing—same as above

Oral communication via business phone and public contact

Research

Creative writing

PRACTICAL ARTS

Laundry Care

Nutrition

Care & responsibility for pets

Care of environment

Cooking & Baking

SCIENCE

Botany (garden)

Dolphins—new research on intelligence and societal make-up

Acid Rain

Waste Management

Volcanoes

Motor repair and maintenance

Electronics Kit and Components Experiment #47

Leukemia testing

PHYSICAL EDUCATION

Bike riding

Basketball

Aerobic exercise (at Humane Society)

OTHER

Respect for elders

Death related to pet over-population

Classical music

Art and hands-on experience an integral portion of most activities

OTHER LANGUAGE

American Sign Language

One day's activity! Accomplished in the warm, loving, safe environment of home! No bells, no tests, no peer pressure, no competition! Individual attention, individual progress, individual choice! The art of education—pure, stressless, naturally occurring. Imagine what can be accomplished in the course of a year.

Take a few more minutes, close your eyes and picture a similar day, plugging in activities you can imagine fitting your children's interests and available where you live. Let your imagination fly.

Welcome back—hope you had a wonderful trip! But please don't think your trip was merely an excursion to a fantasy land. Your exercise sheds light on some very important truths about education. You see the role of teacher can be transformed into that of guide, a facilitator who, by virtue of your natural connection to your children, possesses a unique knowledge of the student. Devoting a relatively short period of time, initially, to observation, you can tune in to the ways in which your child learns best, help her pursue interests, honor her strengths, shore up her weaknesses and participate, side by side, in a most interesting learning journey.

You discover every day life tosses you umpteen opportunities for learning, if only your child experiences it guided by a loving adult. You see there is time enough for yourself, as well as time to guide the child you birthed, if only you are willing to take that time away from less important pursuits. You see love and connection more than compensate for formal "training," if only you rise above your conditioning to the contrary and allow that understanding to blossom into trust of self and child. You realize that as a place "to learn," to acquire lasting, meaningful, universal life skills, home is a *very good*, "radically novel idea."

> You may say I'm a dreamer
> But I'm not the only one.
> I hope some day you'll join us...
>   John Lennon ©1971

CHAPTER ELEVEN

COPING WITH BEING A PIONEER ON THE ROAD TO FREEDOM

Granpa said some nations was uppity in the same way and would give and give so they could call theirselves big shots, when if they had their heart in the right place, would learn the people to who they was giving how to do for theirselves. Granpa said these nations wouldn't do this because then the other people would not be dependent on them, and that's what they was after in the first place.

—Forrest Carter, in *The Education of Little Tree*

P lease notice this section isn't plain ol' "Coping with Freedom." I harbor no illusions that family centered education alone will make all Americans truly free. Family centered education can, however, point your family in the direction toward achieving the personal promise of life, liberty, and the pursuit of happiness originally envisioned when this nation was founded.

Family centered education will not immediately correct "politics as usual" or cause the destructive patterns of public schools that lead us away from freedom to cease. But by claiming responsibility for your own children and your mutual education, you can *learn to be free* in thought, word, and deed in the privacy of your own environment.

Family centered education lets you "step away" from deep involvement in the status quo. Maybe it fulfills the "detachment" spiritual leaders throughout the ages have taught, the detachment that would benefit society if more of us practiced it in at least one aspect of our lives. The revelations that occur naturally with that first step lead you to "step away" from other arenas in the status quo. They allow you to become conscious of activities around you that usually go unheard, unnoticed, unquestioned. It is like waking up from a long, drugged sleep. "Stepping away" lets you see things with fresh, new eyes.

Fresh, new eyes are capable of seeing that the best place to discover freedom is within yourself. None of the institutions that dominate our country—the economy, the government, organized religion, the schools—can allow freedom and expect to maintain the status quo. That's OK. Because just like all other learning, the lessons of freedom lie in experiencing it. And when you experience freedom (as opposed to reading about it or considering it a lofty ideal only dreamers aspire to) you have true freedom, that which radiates from within. Rather than waiting for someone to bestow external freedom on you (your institutions will keep you waiting for eternity!), you lay claim to the freedom that always exists inside.

Independence. Truly learning how to do for ourselves. This freedom is freedom of spirit.

> Cherish therefore the spirit of our people and keep alive their attention. Do not be severe upon their errors, but reclaim them by enlightening them. If once they become inattentive to public affairs, you and I and Congress and Assemblies, judges and governors, shall all become wolves.
>
> —Thomas Jefferson (in 1787 letter to Edward Carrington)

The Fallacy of Freedom in America

> A right is not what someone gives you; it's what no one can take from you.
>
> —Former U.S. Attorney General Ramsey Clark
> in *The New York Times*, October 2, 1977

Here in the "land of the free," we dealt a blow to the most literal form of bondage when Lincoln freed the slaves. No more would there arise such a blatant violation of an American man's right to pursue liberty. The double standard piercing equality of all men disappeared. (For simplicity's sake you have to forget that women weren't included in this discussion.)

This view of freedom carries boatloads of refugees to American shores, for the call sounds loudly in the hearts of humankind no matter where they happen to be born. It's the same notion of freedom protecting our speech, press, right to assemble, bear arms and choose a personally acceptable religion.

This is the way we normally think of American freedom, related to physical activity and movement within society. It's the idea of American freedom permeating classroom lectures from Maine to California. But just as the idea of true education moves beyond teachers and classrooms, so can the idea of freedom transcend the mere physical aspect of humanity. Let's first take a closer look at the definition of *freedom*, again compliments of *The American Heritage Dictionary of the English Language:* When we get past the typical, physical connotation, we find "Liberty of the person from slavery, oppression, or incarceration," and further on "immunity from the arbitrary exercise of authority," as well as "the capacity to exercise choice; free will."

Anyone who has attended public school has not spent her life free of "arbitrary exercise of authority." If you are one of millions of parents today *asking* for choice in education, you do not possess "the capacity to exercise free choice" or you wouldn't be asking your legislators to give it to you!

But let's move beyond these obvious examples of the fallacy of freedom. Lincoln freed Americans from slavery, and in so doing bestowed a sense of equality. But what about oppression? The same dictionary says oppression is "a feeling of being heavily weighed down, either mentally or physically; depression; weariness." Aren't these the symptoms of what those in politically correct circles term psychological illness? And aren't there a frighteningly huge amount of people seeking counseling and/or taking drugs for these symptoms?

One might say Americans are not suffering from migraines, depression, the weight of stress (mental *and* physical), burn-out, and behavior disorders of all shapes and sizes, most obvious in our culture in the form of addictions like gambling, eating, not eating, sex, shopping, making money, power, etc., etc. Americans could be said to be suffering the symptoms of oppression.

If that's the case, we don't need to sink into further dependence on "experts" or counselors who merely put Band-Aids on our tumor. We need true freedom—independence—in a dose large enough to wipe out the symptoms' root cause—oppression.

Oppression of spirit is not on the public school curriculum. Rather, it is a noxious by-product produced while stewing schooling in a pot with unions, administrators, multi-billion dollar budgets, state education departments, and school boards, then letting politicians control the heat.

Americans have equality (at least in the law books), in large part because equality has long been an important issue here, noticed in 1835 by de Tocqueville, a French statesmen who observed America and Americans before writing *Democracy in America*: "Americans are so enamored of equality that they would rather be equal in slavery than unequal in freedom."[1] American interest in and acquisition of "equality" overshadowed the deeper, more meaningful aspect of true freedom, freedom of spirit, in part because we have, as Jefferson feared, "become inattentive to public affairs."

And just as Jefferson warned, over time many of the politically elite transformed into wolves. Our institutions, including education, roll on dominated by the politicians' pack (and today's "PACs," political action committees, of various species, as well). Public inattention makes oppression so doggone easy; it's simply a matter of conditioning masses of young chicks while no one stands guard over the hen house.

> There is no "slippery slope" toward loss of liberties, only a long staircase where each step downward must first be tolerated by the American people and their leaders.
> — U. S. Senator Alan K. Simpson
> in *The New York Times,* Sept. 26, 1982

Our one-style-fits-all education approach oppresses spirit. Its grasp constantly grows larger and stronger in spite of its standing as America's well-fortified, covert, antithesis to freedom. The National Education Goals have been signed into law by President Clinton. (The fact that you won't find the subject of education anywhere in the Constitution, which means it is the province of the state and the people, doesn't stop the President from signing a law containing the "carrots" that ensure "voluntary compliance" from states, communities, and parents.) The federal U. S. Department of Education has enough money and power to utilize mass communication through the technology of computers, has immediate access to every school in the nation, and produces a monthly newsletter free to anyone requesting it: *Community Update,* 1-800-USA-LEARN. It's a quick and cheap way to keep you moving toward waking up, aware, at the very least, of the mindset of the pursestring-controlling federal government. While you're at it, also ask for a copy of "Goals 2000: Educate America Act." Mine came with a form cover letter addressed to "Community Activist." (Call NOW—I promise I'll wait!)

The U.S. Department of Education also provides "Satellite Town Meetings." (Personally I think this phrase is an oxymoron. Only a minute fraction of the audience can take part in a "satellite" meeting. At a "town" meeting, however, anyone with something to say is usually guaranteed to be heard.) February '94's Satellite Town

Meeting was sponsored by Miles, Inc. and Metropolitan Life, and the U.S. Chamber of Commerce cooperated with the production end.

We've been promised that Secretary of Education "Riley's Rules" are forthcoming (in the form of "simple but helpful advice on education for parents"), along with a series of close examination papers, the first devoted to "the role of parents," of course.

When President Clinton submitted the *Goals 2000: Educate America Act to Congress,* his cover letter included this: "States have always been the 'laboratories of democracy.' This has been especially true in education over the past decades. The lessons we have learned from the collective work of States, local education agencies, and individual schools are incorporated in Goals 2000..."

Stop a minute, Bill. 1) *If* methods and/or curriculum worked at the state, local, and individual school level, that means they worked without interference from the federal government. The federal government has an uncanny way of throwing a wrench into anything that succeeds before they get their hands on it. 2) Many of the lessons learned by home educators work on a personal level, like winter-snuggling-under-the-blanket-to-read-a-book, among other things. Home can't be duplicated in institutionalized classrooms, and community level success can't be guaranteed and/or duplicated at the federal level. 3) The lessons you claim you have learned come from seeing education from a totally skewed viewpoint in the first place. But that's why you go on to say: "...and provide the basis for a new partnership between the Federal Government, States, parents, business, labor, schools, communities, and students."

Whoa! Since schools have been working to meet *their* needs, government, business, and labor are already dictatorial "partners" in education. (And remember, if the writers of the Constitution had wanted federal meddling in the art of education they would have said so.) Just as a Satellite Town Meeting can't really be called a town meeting, a partnership between the controllers and the controlled isn't a partnership in the true sense of the word. A *new and improved* partnership would eliminate government, business and labor, and consist only of parents, schools, communities and students. Parents with justifiable concerns, teachers with knowledge of the front lines, and students capable of expressing their needs and desires could be assured of having a voice and making a difference at this level. Here are the only arms in which responsibility for the art of education should rest. It's the only level at which individuals, not institutions, can repair families enough to once again provide the building blocks of aware, safe and responsive communities.

You need only apply minimal common sense to realize that institutionalization, particularly at increasingly younger and younger ages, weighs heavily on a young spirit curious and eager about its environment. By by-passing the institution and practicing the art of education at home, your children can skip the oppression, the weariness, the feeling of mental or physical burdens, and grow with spirits that maintain energy and strength, living a free life.

Coping with being a pioneer on the road to freedom means realizing freedom of spirit amidst many who mistakenly believe they already have it or don't realize it's missing from their lives. At times, this can be an uncomfortable situation, particularly in social circles where school serves as the common denominator among acquaintances who may have very little else in common. Any gathering of parents making small talk inevitably turns to subjects related to school—schedules, tests, complaints, and the problem *du jour.* Once you taste freedom of spirit, you see that the physical and mental manoeuvrings they attempt within the shackles of covert oppression are futile. You can't be included by explaining your freedom to those who have never experienced it, for the description is not the described. Your vision has expanded, and you can't describe peripheral vision to someone who only knows tunnel vision.

As your understanding of freedom and education transform, you, too, will be transformed. Previous assumptions about a society that perpetuates itself through public schooling will open to scrutiny. Many family centered educators reach a point where they can no longer exchange conformity for societal acceptance.

You must eventually learn to be content with your personal evolution, content to be understood only by others who have either experienced freedom of spirit for themselves or are on their own path to freedom. Fortunately more and more of these folks populate your neighborhood and grow increasingly visible in the community.

Don't get discouraged. Remember your individualism creates

more benefit than hardship. Remain joyful that your vision expands, and that your children are growing with free spirits. Just as a pebble dropped in a lake creates waves that ever so gently reach and affect the opposite shore, so too will your family's gift of freedom eventually touch shores that today seem very far away. Be content knowing that you are working in the one place where your work matters most.

> The man who asks of freedom anything other than itself is born to be a slave.
> —A. de Tocqueville (*The Old Regime and the French Revolution*, 1856)

The Buck Stops Here:
Accepting Responsibility and Consequences

> Liberty means responsibility. That is why most men dread it.
> —George Bernard Shaw

Whatever you are thinking about your children's education at this point, one thing should be perfectly clear: Our days of throwing blame for the condition of public school between politicians, teachers, unions, and the schools themselves are over. These folks are either unwilling or unable to create positive change.

If unwilling, the current agenda is suspect and should not be supported, either by money or participation. If unable, then the torch must pass to more capable, caring hands.

There's only one logical place for the buck to stop—in your lap.

Sure, it's heavy. You've never carried this kind of weight before. Yes, it's scary. The unknown always stirs fear and self-doubt. But keeping responsibility for the family's education within the family is the price you pay for freedom of spirit for you and the kids.

When you look at value received for the cost, you'll discover it's really a pretty good deal. Remember, *not* accepting responsibility has a price, too. Allowing others to schedule, plan, and use questionable behaviorist management methods, transmit unexamined values, and even use unapproved oral and body language in your child's daily life can create a dichotomy of character seldom understood, rarely mended. And the most expensive portion of the not-accepting responsibility bill, of course, is giving away family time, the essential tool parents and children need in order to know one another, understand one another, love one another.

According to Dr. T. Berry Brazelton we "are the least family-oriented society in the civilized world." In the civilized world! Mom and Pop take power lunches instead of family picnics. We attend adult, self-help classes instead of library story hour. We read computer print-outs instead of bedtime stories. We are plagued, in epidemic proportion, with a school-induced, social sleeping disease.

It might help if you realize that regardless of the quality or quantity of responsibility you previously delegated to others, you have always been the responsible party, perhaps just too well hidden behind an army of trained government workers to recognize it. Since you are ultimately responsible, doesn't it make sense to accept the responsibility wholeheartedly?

Who is most concerned about your child and her future—the President? The Board of Education? The teacher? The bus driver? Or you? A job accepted by the most caring candidate is likely to be a job best accomplished. Like a craftsman of fine sculpture, you'll approach your role with deep thought and planning, the finest materials, creativity, attention to detail, patience and a gentle, loving touch.

Accepting responsibility is difficult, particularly when you look around and see it's a virtue all but extinct. If no one else is habitually accepting responsibility, you could argue, why should you? The most logical answer is so that you may totally experience responsibility, including suffering the consequences—or rejoicing in them.

We learn our best lessons from our worst mistakes. We lose all those learning opportunities if we let others handle responsibility that is rightfully ours. When you claim mistakes as your own you grow smarter, stronger. You stretch character to the point of flexibility, able to roll with the punches or stand a little straighter and fight a lot harder when those who would flex their muscles try taking responsibility away from you.

We can experience humility through our greatest successes. It sounds paradoxical, but when, with practice, you learn your greatest contribution to your children's education is the fact that you trust enough to get out of the way, you realize they learn and succeed in spite of you, not because of you.

The positive consequences of accepting responsibility in family centered education outnumber the negative, you'll be relieved to know. Where negative consequences stretch character, positive consequences energize and revitalize your spirit as thoughts fill with wonder, days overflow with excitement, and hearts, readily pouring forth love, trust and respect, make room for even more to grow.

Family time fills with oscillating trust. Trust, please realize, is not synonymous with belief (as in "I believe you, son.") Belief is of the mind. Trust is of the heart. Belief and trust exist side by side yet never meet. Believing that you and your children can shoulder responsibility leads you to begin, but it doesn't allow you to relax. By believing you are following the mind and, as you remember, the mind constantly moves from one thought to another, from one text book to another, from one method to another, searching for an ultimate satisfaction that never appears. The mind keeps you on edge, constantly tossed about in a struggle to obtain a goal, whatever you believe in.

In trust there is no struggle. There is acceptance. Some call it surrender. You no longer seek to control your child's education, you simply allow education to occur. When you no longer need to control, you relax. Responsibility happens. Consequences happen. Education happens.

Rather than giving over your mind to the responsibility of family centered education, give over your heart. It will take time and practice, just like every skill does, to develop the ability to allow acceptance of responsibility to flow from the heart instead of the head. The ability will not appear because you think about it, no matter how long or hard you think. It is the very thinking, the constant search of the mind to *justify* responsibility that creates stress and an inability to simply accept it.

Stress blocks all that is good within your heart from ascending as inspired action. The best artists in history always turned attention, time, and devotion to their work, their creativity, freeing them from stress, leaving room for inspiration.

Think of family centered learning in the same light. Give over your heart—your attention, time and devotion. All else, including shoulders strong enough to hold great responsibility, will follow.

You Are So Strange

> Some say I've lost my mind and
> others think I'm crazy!
> While some suggest I stay
> at home because I'm lazy
> I'm happy to tell them,
> "This is most untrue."
> I just changed my career
> When I answered the ad...
> Wanted: Housewife/Mother of two.
> —Barbara Beckett

No doubt about it. When you start announcing to the world that you *want* to stay home with the kids, when you declare their learning experience is more important than the salary you're giving up, when you proclaim that you're actually enjoying it all, somebody, somewhere is going to say, "You are soooo strange." (Or s/he will just think it and verbalize it to a friend later!)

The potential list includes, but is not limited to, friends, fellow workers, clients, neighbors, relatives near and far, grocery store clerks, your children's current teachers, pediatrician, orthodontist, football coach and, perhaps, even your spouse.

Since practically everyone has experienced public school classes or conventional schooling of some sort, our mutual experience is an unofficial group consensus of "normal." When you compare family centered education to "normal," it sticks out like a sore thumb. Neither schooling nor society-at-large provides a handy yardstick by which home education can be measured. Neither schooling nor society-at-large leaves many with the ability to successfully imagine an alternative to institutionalized, classroom experiences.

The art of education, like all art, is basically a private affair. This concept of privacy appears alien in a social climate where kids are encouraged to turn to in-the-same-throes-of-adolescence peers for advice instead of inward for wisdom, where a quick turn of T.V. or radio dial puts you and millions of other viewers in the middle of marital and family dilemmas via "talk shows," and where increasing numbers of parents who attempt legitimate discipline face threats of being turned in to "authorities" for child abuse by children who "know their rights." (These are children receiving the same conditioning as those we met earlier who know they have a "right to be told what to do.") In any comparison to public school relatively little is known about home education. Even less is totally understood. (A well-schooled person who gets paid for doling out advice to others in the role of therapist told me homeschooling was merely a cover for child abuse, representing the most extreme lack of understanding I've personally encountered.)

Most pioneers find that their "march to the beat of a different drummer" is often misconstrued as strange when they set out following their hearts instead of the herd. People laughed as the Wright Brothers worked on their flying machine. Thomas Edison's teacher told his mother he was a dim bulb. Few fellow scientists believed in Albert Einstein's work until enough time passed for his theories to be tested and proved.

Though large numbers of family centered educators have yet to be "tested and proved," University of Michigan assistant professor of education J. Gary Knowles was eager to find out if homeschool critics' major concerns held any water. He set off to ascertain if homeschooled kids could become "productive, participating members of a diverse and democratic society" or were deprived of "normal social development" by studying grown homeschoolers.

Knowles, presenting his findings at a conference in New Zealand, "found no evidence that these adults were even moderately disadvantaged in either respect." None of his respondents were unemployed or on any form of welfare assistance, more than forty percent attended college, and nearly two-thirds were self employed, providing jobs to others or working alongside family members. (Everyone should be so strange, eh?)

Looking back, *ninety-six percent* said they would homeschool again. "Many mentioned the strong relationship it engendered with their parents," Knowles explains, "while others talked about the self-directed curriculum and individualized pace..."

Knowles concludes that "...done in an *enlightened, broadminded* way, with plenty of flexibility in curriculum and methods, homeschooling can be a positive experience for children with benefits that last for many years."[2] (Emphasis added.)

If this type of long-term result makes these grown children and their families "strange," perhaps it's time to inject a dose of the bizarre into the nation's water supplies! Could *your* potential critics who will mistake different for strange also be ignorant of "different's" positive results? Does it really matter what others say or think when the process, as well as the outcome, can serve you, your children, and your community so well?

> Awareness need never remain superficial in an educated man, whereas unawareness is certain to be ignorance probably compounded by arrogance.
> —National Conference on Higher Education, report prepared for annual meeting, Chicago, April 20, 1964

The concept of "strange" as it relates to family centered education is further enforced by our unquestioning acceptance as fact that women are leaving home in droves, seeking bliss and personal fulfillment in service to the American economy instead of in service to her family. Do you think it's at all possible we've been collectively misled regarding what the rest of us do with our time?

Brenda Hunter, Ph.D., author of *Home by Choice: Facing the Effects of Mother's Absence*, calls stay-at-home mothers a "misinformed, intimidated, silent majority." A feminist agenda just one short generation ago transformed the taken-for-granted, unassuming but essential, nurturing mother into front page stories as bra-burning, briefcase toting male equals. (There's that equality instead of freedom again!) These moms soon demanded "quantity" child care, a demand business and government were only too happy to echo, to work for and achieve. (More workers! More taxes! More time to condition even younger children!) Liberated women's new and increasing economic needs quickly overshadowed those of women who chose to stay in bras and backyards. They stole the nation's attention and support from families the way a pit bull steals food from a poodle. Working women—a new market generating new businesses to serve new priorities—turned motherhood into a secondary activity accomplished in one's spare time. Moreover, they left non-income-producing women feeling more and more like anachronisms.

Those all-important statistics regarding working women highlighted in magazines, newspapers, and television seem to support the new view and prove out-of-home mom as normal. But when two American Enterprise Institute scholars dissected the Department of Labor and U.S. Census Bureau data, more precise information emerged. The working mother as majority, on closer inspection, appears to be yet another cultural lie.

At a time we were told sixty-two percent of mothers of children under eighteen were working, it turns out only forty-one percent of *all* mothers were full-timers. For mothers of children under six, this full-time figure dropped to thirty-three percent. To distort things just a little more, the Department of Labor classifies any and all *temporary*, full-time work as "mothers working full time," even if her foray into business lasts only a month.

When mothers are classified even *more* clearly, nuclear family (both parents live at home with the kids) moms are *home* full or part-time in sixty-one percent of the households! The higher percentage of working moms we've grown accustomed to hearing about occurs with divorced moms (63%), but what we're not usually told is that divorced moms constitute only eleven percent of the total of working moms.[3]

If you have inner urgings to be with your children, if you don't feel quite right about granting responsibility for their lives and learning to others, if you feel that your role as mother is more precious than the ability to buy a bigger house or have a place on the economic merry-go-round or advance your own education, *you are not strange!* Despite the propaganda to the contrary, the traditional family, although quietly and purposefully ignored, still has a pulse, even though its prognosis is uncertain in these very trying times.

Let go of the belief you must act contrary to your inner feelings simply because you think you're out of step with the rest of your culture. Know that you can live by feminist principles without succumbing to others' programs for life. Realize that increasing pressures on mothers to join the work force do not serve the best interest of family or, in the long run, society. The increasing problems of this country's children make it abundantly clear that our recent cultural experiment in allowing strangers to raise children—or worse, leaving children alone to raise themselves—is a tragic failure.

If it only took us one generation to wreak such havoc, we can clean things up in the same length of time. If families follow their hearts instead of the economy's carrots, our children *will* follow our lead. When we reach "critical mass," when enough of us come out of the closet and declare our "strangeness," the label *will* vanish. Just like the bras—in a puff of smoke.

Running Into Walls

So here you are, standing on the brink of changing family priorities, altering your family's schedule and lifestyle, feeling alone, "strange," and vulnerable. You step gingerly onto the road to freedom, wondering what the heck you're doing here alone. Inching along slowly, you gather courage and trust like a tiny but growing bouquet of wildflowers when BAM! you run, nose first, into a wall blocking your path.

What is the wall made of? It could be anything—one of those people that think you're strange, a school superintendent, a school board, homeschool "experts," your pocketbook, in fortunately diminishing instances, the law, or even your own thoughts.

Whatever the wall is made of doesn't really matter in this discussion. The point is *any* wall will produce *x* amount of pain. Any wall can stop you dead in your tracks as you rub your nose and ask over and over again, "What am I doing?!"

Whatever the wall is made of doesn't really matter because you realize a wall by any name (in-law, state law, friend, pocketbook, pediatrician, superintendent) will still be a wall. But there are alternatives to smacking your nose against the wall if you get creative with your thinking. If you can't go through it, go over it. If you can't go over it, go around it. If you can't go around it, go under it. In other words, think alternatively. Take another route, often the one less traveled, to keep the wall from stopping you. In other words, you must think alternatively in order to put alternatives into action.

It's great exercise for muscles grown stiff and lazy from lack of use. When you use an arm in only one way, it hurts too much to use it differently. Different use equals pain, and the arm shoots back to its narrow comfort zone. It won't do that again!

But if you get that arm's muscles "thinking" in different directions through slow, steady exercise, the muscles grow more flexible, stronger. With patience and practice, the arm "goes around" the pain until the pain dissolves, just as the walls will.

Guess you could say that's the good news about walls. They get you thinking in directions you might not have considered if they weren't there. And let's face it, our society works in such a way as to keep building a good number of walls in the paths of those seeking to trot toward freedom. You get lots of exercise.

Though regulations are not actually laws, all states have either. And both limit to varying degrees the free practice of education. Always remember pertinent laws vary from state to state, therefore the requirements change, slightly or dramatically, among the states. You'll need to check with a support group (recommended) or your state department of education (not recommended but will suffice if all else fails) to get a copy of those pertaining to your area to see to what degree your state regulates. If you have a family move in your future, it would be wise to consider the new location's rules about home education in your decision-making process. As you might expect, homeschoolers report difficulty moving *to* a more restrictive state, while they find a move *from* a restrictive state a very liberating experience. And even if homeschooling is just a maybe in your future, it's a plus to plant your family where it has the best chance to flourish.

In spite of (or because of) family centered education's 15-20% annual growth over the last decade[4], and the benefits for children evident everywhere from research to personal accounts to test scores, the education establishment cannot find it in their hearts to give this alternative its blessings. The education institution is an example of a very large wall, not ready to tumble anytime soon. A good illustration of an obstructionist attitude is reflected in Section C-40 of the 1993-1994 Resolution of the NEA: "The National Education Association believes that home education programs cannot provide the student with a comprehensive education experience. The Association believes that, if parental preference home schooling study occurs, students enrolled must meet all state requirements. Instruction should be by persons who are licensed by the appropriate state agency, and a curriculum approved by the state department of education should be used."

This statement from the nation's largest union (2.1 million members)[5] displays their thirst for control by voicing their desire to have family centered educators duplicate their own practices via state-licensed teachers and "approval" of one's curriculum. Is this to help more families find happiness and educational success as they practice an alternative to the establishment's methods? Or to ensure their own perpetuation? Read this response to a June '93 *Forbes* report uncovering the constitutionally questionable practices of the NEA from a Washington, D. C. NEA headquarters employee: "Your portrayal of NEA was quite accurate. In fact, it may have been too kind...NEA maintains a management hierarchy of tyrants and bullies who are vicious, malicious, and relentless in their pursuit of control."

The other walls you'll encounter aren't as large or politically powerful as the NEA and state departments of education, but they require even more dexterity and alternative thinking when you meet them because they exist on a more personal level. None of the walls are closer to you or able to stop you as quickly as your own negative thoughts.

There may be times when thoughts of incapability or other negatives stand as barriers between you and your next step toward reclaiming your self, your family, and your community through family centered education. Keep just one important fact in the forefront of your heart and mind if this happens:

There are no magic formulas to guarantee your success. The walls will be there; it is up to you to give your alternative thinking muscles a work-out and discover which of the many options at your disposal is the best way to overcome the obstructions. Like long-distance runners who keep their bodies in top form so they're ready to hit the wall, then move beyond the pain to reach the finish line, you will keep patience, flexibility, creativity, and trust in top form.

You, who change thousands of stinky diapers, kiss away scores of dirty cuts and bruises, awake nightly for 3 A.M. feedings, repeatedly clean mashed bananas off the kitchen cabinets, and run yourself ragged alongside a wobbly, beginning bicycle rider possess everything you need—and much more.

When you run into those inevitable walls, don't look for tried and true formulas—find your own magic.

PART TWO

Benefits of the Art

Something we were withholding made us weak
Until we found it was ourselves.

—Robert Frost

Obstacles to the practice of the art of education, to reclaiming your family, your community, and your Self in public schools *or* at home, may seem insurmountable after our brief review of the size and power of the institutions and their influences across our culture.

Can your children really grow into free-thinking individuals eagerly pursuing a potential-filling path toward responsible, caring adulthood?

Can your family really double, triple, even quadruple time together, allowing bonds of love and respect to strengthen?

Can your community really become a "classroom without walls" where learning is a natural, joy-filled process overflowing with win-win benefits for all involved?

Can you really guide your own children in an education worth having, gaining valuable insights and what likely will be your first *true* education in the process?

Can you really achieve all these things by accepting the responsibility of family centered education?

Yes.
All these. And much, much more.

You know better than anyone where life thus far has taken you. And I realize that imagining a different path for your growing family is a definite challenge. So to help you meet that challenge, you need a peek at the benefits of family centered education, benefits that reach far beyond those often cited in newspaper and magazine reports that focus almost exclusively on home-educated children's academic successes. The areas covered are not all-inclusive, for individual families discover new benefits every day, and each contracts or expands its wings depending on its special circumstances.

As you explore these benefits, feel free to stretch your wings and make a list of further advantages your truly unique family could realize. Forget the limits you normally place on your thoughts and, therefore, your abilities. Come along and open up to the possibilities that lie ahead.

CHAPTER TWELVE

BENEFITS FOR YOU

I AM THE CAPTAIN OF MY SOUL

> Don't let what you're being get in the way of what you might become.
>
> —Harry Palmer

You Can See Clearly Now

My initial reasons for entering the world of home-schooling revolved solely around my children. I saw an opportunity to spare them from spending many adult years shaking off the conditioning that would limit their thinking, their potential, and their happiness. My oldest child's brief stint in public school kindergarten had already revealed 1) the stress of too-early formal book learning, 2) the behavior-altering effects of peer pressure, 3) the personality-altering effects of school "discipline," 4) the spirit-altering effects of boredom, irrelevance, separation, etc., etc.

I decided to bite the bullet and "sacrifice" my time to this scary, almost revolutionary approach to raising a family, all the while thinking how noble and self-sacrificing the act would be. Little did I realize how wonderful an awakening lay right around the corner of my own life.

As the children acquired basic skills—reading, writing, arithmetic—their interests expanded. So did mine. Their sense of wonder blossomed. So did mine. Their abilities multiplied. So did mine. Their confidence increased. So did mine.

The true meaning of education, courtesy of the examples right under my nose, grew clearer every day. The subject of education, I soon realized, was worthy of further study and, more importantly, deep contemplation. I dove into my first "interest-initiated" learning experience void of a prepared curriculum or teacher but fully attentive. I learned how to learn.

Within a relatively short period of time I discovered I was bringing the same reasoning, contemplation, and freedom of inquiry to other areas of concern in my life. "Teaching" my kids at home brought universal life skills into sharp focus. Awareness increased. Consciousness increased (with guidance from other areas of study and contemplation).

This side-benefit to the "teacher" in family centered education—awakened consciousness to environmental forces (including social forces) that affect your family's day-to-day life—harbors major potential for societal change as it naturally multiplies within the family. Children growing in close proximity to an adult experiencing growing consciousness reap the benefits early in life. They, in turn, take this awareness out into their world, touching the lives of others. One day they will pass it on to their children. The potential is unlimited; the implications exciting. Here is an opportunity for you, feeling unable to fix a society sorely in need of improvement all by yourself, to truly make a difference on a scale you and your family can manage at home.

You don't need millions of dollars or political influence to repair the damage you see around you. Granted, we as a nation are far from realizing the "critical mass" of folks it will take to restore true freedom and equality in America. But if, as quantum physicists are saying, "The key to understanding the universe is you," so, too, the key to the freedom and wholeness necessary for significant life, liberty, and the pursuit of happiness is *you*.

Grab the bull by the horns. Wholeheartedly accept responsibility for yourself and your family. Question and, when necessary, refuse the "help" of institutions bent on creating and perpetuating infantile dependency. Your freedom and heightened consciousness will provide you these life-altering advantages:

1) *Giant steps toward personal fulfillment*—Once you answer the question "Who am I?" by stripping away the conditioning of your past in preparation of accepting responsibility, understanding of your *real* Self frees you to follow your own internal callings. By honoring your calling (sometimes called an "inner voice"), you set upon Life's most rewarding journey, at the same time serving as a most inspirational example, the most believable and readily available guide, for your children.

2) *Balance, or wholeness*—No matter whether your family centered education allows you partial or complete freedom from values, pursuits, and time schedules arranged by others, you will find you are quite capable of controlling your own destiny. No longer obligated to act for others' convenience, you find your own rhythm, just as your children discover theirs. You are free to listen to your heart, to create a schedule for living that serves *your* needs (or to avoid schedules completely!). As external callings decrease or disappear according to your needs, you possess the time to

attend to mind, body, and spirit as necessary. Every aspect of your life benefits from the balance, or wholeness, that results.

3) *Abundant choices*—When once you experience the reality of many ways to learn, you'll see there are also abundant lifestyle options available to you and your family. The singular, rigid cycle prescribed by the education institution—school as path to job, job as path to materialism, materialism as path to necessarily increased earnings, necessarily increased earnings as path to increased tax payments, increased tax payments as path to larger government, larger government as path to greater control of our time, our thoughts, our money, our families and our schools—is one you *can* skip *if you choose to.*

When old priorities ruled your life, lifestyle options were few. With family centered education, a whole world of possibilities opens before you as your family's time—your very lives—become, as they should, yours to direct.

You Know Your Kids... And Like Them!

"Although many of first-grader Betsy [Goldman's] friends think learning at home is a great idea, many mothers tell Goldman, 'I couldn't stand being with my kids all day.'"[1]

This same sentiment has laced many a conversation I've had with mothers whose reaction to my declaration that I *enjoy* spending so much time with my children is half amusement, half skepticism. How, I see them wondering, could any 1990's mother subject herself to what, in their perception, is a life filled with the needs, demands, and pettiness of youngsters, void of the rewards (financial *and* ego-stroking) of life in the work force?

What this commonly held misperception fails to take into account is that needful, demanding, petty behavior patterns are very often created by scientific behavior modification training used by the public education institution. (Imagine Dr. Frankenstein's monster here.) Parents, particularly mothers, who voice this common judgment fail to see that children's irritating behavior is a consequence of programming designed, not for the benefit of the children, but for the convenience of the institution. Internal messages constantly whisper to your child, "Be yourself!"

External messages consistently bellow, "Conform!" These mixed messages create confusion and, ultimately, conflict in children too young to reason or to defend themselves. Now you've got behavior parents would rather not witness, thank you very much.

Remove your child from daily behavior modification, free him from external messages that contradict and drown out his internal voice and, eventually, behavior changes. Provide time, your own life, and the lives of variously aged guides and friends as examples and, soon, your needy, demanding, petty child becomes a self-motivated, self-responsible, kinder individual—the kind of person with whom anyone would like to spend time. And that includes you!

If something's "wrong" with our children, we needn't look far beyond their immediate environment to discover the source of many of the problems. In *Whole Child/Whole Parent*, Polly Berrien-Berends reminds parents that "[children's] behavior is like a windsock indicating the direction of our own attention." This is so hard to see when there are too many influences blowing that windsock in too many directions.

Family centered learners simply enjoy spending lots of time with their children. No joke. The patience you think they possess is certainly a virtue, but it's a practiced one. It's practiced more at the beginning of the homeschooling journey, I think, when all concerned are stumbling over uncharted life paths. Then a strange thing happens: Just as you build patience to a peak you never thought you were capable of reaching, you don't need it anymore. For at the same time, you become aware that *that which already exists within your children is far richer, more beautiful, and more important than anything you or the schools have been unsuccessfully trying to create.*

As you settle into family centered education, you will not be spending lots of time with kids you can't stand being around. The time you spend together away from school's behavior modification allows your kids to get to know themselves as the real people they are, the "new" people you also get to know. And respect. And trust. And like!

Our children are the most constant source of wonder, joy, and love in our lives today. Each step of their journey toward independence strengthens our mutual trust, increases shared respect, and daily builds new understanding of what it means to cooperate, to support, to be a member of the first and most important social building block—the family.

> *"Too bad you can't be a kid again and go to college, Mommy,"* she said.
> *"Grown-ups can go to college, too."*
> *"They can? Well, you could go once a week, then."*
> *"No, I'd rather write and be with you kids as you grow up. I still might go, someday."*
> *"Like when I'm 16?"*
> *"Something like that."*
> *"We could go together! I'll talk to the teacher and ask if we can sit next to each other."*
> *"And we could keep learning together."*
> *"Yeah. If you don't know what 4 + 4 is, I could tell you. Mommy, that would really be nice."*

You Get Another Education Free of Charge

If you're feeling ill at ease with the conditioning you received under the guise of an education, if you want to experience learning as the joyful process you intuit it can be, take heart. Family centered education provides you, the parent, the unprecedented opportunity and time to get an education all over again—your way, and free of charge!

My children have filled my life with questions from the moment they began speaking: How? What? When? Where? And my favorite, why?

The search for answers to their questions (and my own) still takes me on a magical learning journey I would never have ventured upon were it not for family centered education. The "post-school" education I continue to receive is the most interesting learning I've ever stumbled upon.

Home educators approach learning from myriad angles. Can't stand the idea of "teaching" math from repetitive drill? There are dominoes, playing cards, Cuisenaire rods, and Popsicle sticks. Or make-believe (or real) checking accounts, trips to the grocery store, and countless board and computer games. Some families use biographies to flow through history, history to discover geography, and geography to enter the world of foreign culture. Science and art *can* walk hand-in hand, as can writing and music, or whatever else interests you.

Study and explore *your* way, right along with the kids while they are still young and find just about any subject—presented in an interesting way—exciting. They will eventually branch off on their own paths, as will you. In the meantime, all of you uncover the unadulterated joy of learning for learning's sake, and carry it forward to future pursuits.

Many parents jump into home education sure that they will share their superior knowledge and serve as teacher in the family centered experience. If this is what you're thinking, you're in for a big surprise!

Through time spent with my kids one thing became perfectly clear: Children have more to teach us than we could ever fool ourselves into thinking we have to teach them. Our children have taught me to let go, to strip away the conditioning like so many winter garments to find the truth of Self. They taught me this merely by being themselves—no games, no ulterior motives, no need to impress or *be* impressed. No desires, no unfulfilled wishes. Their sun warmed my soul and left me feeling totally human once more, a feeling I had surrendered to experts and authorities long before my high school graduation. We experience life together as a family, a school, and as friends, sharing time as learning companions.

> Grown men may learn from very little children for the hearts of little children are pure and, therefore, the Great Spirit may show to them many things which older people miss.
>
> —Black Elk

The education you receive as you learn with your children has no monetary cost, no monetary return. You merely exchange courage and trust for a life experience that fits your family like a glove.

Time Is On My Side

Many folks ask family centered educators typical questions—

typical in regard to "normal" thinking occurring in a schooled mind.

"How much time do you spend homeschooling?"

Time. In reality time does not even exist, yet, it's the ruler by which we measure success and failure, or as we more typically term them, "quality" time and "goofing off" time. When we need to count minutes, to check the hour hand of the clock as it drags one day or flies the next, we've missed the point. The point is not to cut non-existent time into manageable chunks that serve our perceived needs. Rather, family centered education allows you, together as a family, to embrace each moment as it unfolds.

Your stomach can tell you when it's time for a meal. Your body can tell you when it's time to lay down for rest or wake to face the joy of a new day. Your spirit can tell you when it's time to stop and go inside for the light and love you need to bring to the rest of your life.

You need not rush your children to a school bus that also bears the illegitimate message, "After this trip, it's a predetermined time to learn." Every moment of every day is the moment to learn. Each moment presents new and exciting possibilities that are yours for the taking if only you are aware they exist.

The gift of time inherent in family centered education—the time you share with your children—is a unique opportunity in a society constantly forcing you to spend time in a thousand other directions. But it's an opportunity you must present to yourself, by yourself, for yourself. Strong, misguided societal pulls in other directions, like school and the economic merry-go-round, don't allow the time necessary for this opportunity. A lot of folks will be quite happy if you let this opportunity slip by. They'll be ecstatic if you never even realize it exists.

But it does exist. Right here. Right now. It is up to you to begin.

Make your own rules about time. I guarantee your rules will be more comfortable, like a warm pair of slippers on a chilly December evening. Your rules won't assign arbitrary schedules to your family's life, as schedules imposed on you by others must, of necessity, be arbitrary. Your schedule can be a more natural one, serving a purpose in your unique life.

Politicians bemoan the state of U. S. education, yet they continually fail to make the connection between family and true learning, between love and the ability to love, between time together and connection. Do you *really* want someone else to "watch" your children grow as they struggle under the weight of coming of age in a time when every turn around the corner holds decisions they are unprepared to make? Or do you want to actually "raise" your children, physically and in consciousness? If so, family centered education gives you the "time." You can give it back to your family.

> *The homeschooled child missed one multiple choice answer on the math application section of the year-end, fourth grade achievement test. The problem concerned a clock, and the measurement of time. Certainly the problem was age-appropriate, technically appropriate, even culturally appropriate. Unfortunately, it just wasn't his-life-appropriate.*

Family centered education needn't consume "time" to the degree that public school currently eats up your children's time. So much more is efficiently accomplished in a warm, responsive atmosphere as you interact throughout the day. Even single working parents are finding they can earn a living and still have enough time to enjoy the learning journey with their children.

As you realize the connection between life and learning, your fears about not having enough time to "do school" fade away. You can find the time. You can make the time. And if you're really lucky, you can do away with time!

The Question of Money

How much does it cost to homeschool?

As much as you can afford.

Like everything else about family centered education, the amount of money you put into it is flexible. Spend what you can, but don't let a lack of "disposable income" stop you. Unlike school budgets, your budget can reflect a more realistic return on the dollar. When you hear reporters like Thomas McArdle say in *Investor's Business Daily*, "The results of home schooling are startlingly positive,"[2] or public school advocates like Martin Luther King III tell a convention crowd that "homeschooling can be a laboratory for testing new educational methods that can benefit full educational institutions,"[3] you might mistakenly think these families spend a lot of money on education.

Don't let your local school budget fool you. It doesn't take thousands of dollars per student to get a true education—it only takes thousands of dollars per student to run an education institution. You're not running an institution. Because your investment directly benefits your children, a little money goes a lot further. If the cost of correspondence school or a curriculum is prohibitive, you can get by without them. If you think you'd feel better (at least at the starting gate) with a prepared curriculum, read Borg Hendrickson's *How to Write a Low Cost/No Cost Curriculum* and start *your* true education with learning how to set your own path toward knowledge.

Use your community library as the heart of your sources and connection to an ever-growing network of information. A public library, open to all on an equal basis and still offering many services free in spite of escalating costs, is our society's last link to free inquiry and the first link to the much-needed community learning centers of the future. (See Chapter 14 for more on learning centers.)

The Public Library Association's Parent Education Services Committee took the time to study home educators. Their findings appear in *Homeschoolers and the Public Library: A Resource Guide for Libraries Serving Homeschoolers.* Perhaps librarians are recognizing family centered learners as the fastest growing group of Americans who truly appreciate and utilize these community facilities as the valuable assets they are. Whatever the reason, librarians see that "this conventional educational alternative has become a reality with which our educational system must deal realistically and cooperatively." (OK, I can't help myself and have to say it here: Whether you decide to homeschool or not, *please* support your community library with your presence and your money, and use its resources to your family's benefit!)

You can also keep the cost of education low by scouring library book sales and those backbones of American culture, garage sales. One man's trash often turns out to be a homeschooler's treasure as you build your own library. Classic literature doesn't change whether you spend $15.95 in a bookstore or 25¢ on a neighbor's front lawn! The same goes for many reference books, particularly

history books (including biographies), nature books (encyclopedias and guide books), or dictionaries, thesauruses, writing
guides, atlases, maps, and many art books. While you're out bar-
gain hunting, don't forget to look for materials that creative young
minds can turn into works of art! You can also find old electric
typewriters, adding machines, record players (we found a Victrola
that came with a record collection including Warren G. Harding
speeches, "General Pershing's March," French music, and other
wonderful examples of 1900's musical entertainment), old clocks
(to be torn apart, examined, and maybe even repaired), games
(cheap enough to take the markers, dice, money and/or cards and
create a new game), and much more.

Don't forget loans of material from family, friends, and homeschooling support groups. Whenever our support group gets
together, kids' books, cassettes, and games rapidly exchange
hands. That's not to mention the clothes, recipes, foodstuff, animal
cages, and myriad other materials that get traded, bought, or given
away.

Home education doesn't have to cost a lot of money if you substitute creativity and ingenuity for greenbacks. But then there *is*
the question of living without a second source of income to which
your family may have become very accustomed.

I've always considered finances a personal matter, so I don't
intend to provide you with a sure-fire way to make do. While
"Examining Priorities," you may have uncovered ideas to help
you learn to live with less. I'll include in the appendix a list of
newsletters chock-full of ways to further help you trim the family's
budget. But here are a few "savings" you can't enjoy *until* you kiss
that second paycheck goodbye and dive into family centered education. Let the list help you put "lost" money in a truer perspective:

1) *Income tax bills*— It's quite possible you'll see more of the
money from the pay check you hang onto to provide more for your
family instead of for the government. Don't forget to check this
angle of hidden savings when making calculations.

2) *Clothing*—Figure out what you normally spend on looking
good for work and keeping your kids in the latest fashions to keep
up with their peers at school. Home educators can get by with

minimal wardrobes and use that clothing money in more meaningful directions.

3) *Transportation*—A portion of that lost income went to getting you to work, either by car or mass transportation.

4) *Meals away from home*—It's a lot cheaper to lunch at home on a bowl of soup teeming with vegetables from your own garden than it is to join your co-workers at even a relatively inexpensive fast food joint every afternoon.

5) *Health costs*—If you're currently suffering from any job-related stress or physical ailments, soon your doctor may no longer consider you one of his best patients. Your children are much less likely to pick up every germ that travels at the speed of light through local classrooms. Flu and chicken pox epidemics might miss your entire family! And don't forget that schools are waiting until laws force them to provide lunches lower in fat, higher in fresh produce content. You can serve healthier lunches immediately because you *want* to, not because you *have* to.

6) *Entertainment*—Lots of families caught in the school/job whirlpool have to make a concerted effort to provide "quality" time for the family, which oftentimes involves the expenses associated with "going somewhere" and "doing something" together. Once you spend more time together, your need for this will likely decline. Entertainment can marry education and become edutainment, a delightful blend of fun and learning accomplished through low cost/no cost activities within your community.

7) *Child care*—This frequently bites a large chunk of a second pay check. Figure out how much you spend for someone else to watch the kids, a part of which you might now spend *on* the kids.

There are other expenses involved in earning a paycheck depending upon your job. Once you've added them all up, you'll have a clearer picture of how much money you'll actually lose by giving up your family's second income. And given all the benefits family centered education provides you, "losing" some money may not be as devastating as you've been led to believe it is.

If you find a second income is necessary to your situation, don't give up. Large numbers of homeschooling families are joining the ranks of one of the largest economic movements in this country— the home-based business. The same creativity, courage and trust you utilize in educating your own children can also free you from dependence on external paychecks.

By conducting money-making activities from home, you control the work load and the work hours. You can custom design your business to fit your lifestyle. Best of all, conducting business under your own roof creates learning opportunities for your kids that wouldn't otherwise exist. When you're the boss, your children don't just visit the workplace. They help, they learn, and they realize, via yet another avenue, that they are an important part of a team.

There are many ways to make home education a financially realistic option for your family. When it comes to the question of money, the answer is "think creatively!"

If you've read any of the newspaper or magazine articles, or watched any of the television news coverage on home education, you've already discovered that homeschooled children, as a group, realize academic achievement equal to or better than their conventionally schooled counterparts. But there are many more—and more important—advantages to family centered education ahead for your children. If you haven't looked beyond the obvious improved test scores, you're in for a real surprise. Let's take a look at the benefits homeschoolers report can make your children's lives happier and more meaningful.

CHAPTER THIRTEEN

BENEFITS FOR YOUR CHILDREN

SUFFER THE LITTLE CHILDREN TO COME UNTO ME

Children are given to us—on loan—for a very short period of time. They come to us like packets of flower seeds, with no pictures on the cover and no guarantees. We do not know what they will look like, act like, or have the potential to become. Our job, like the gardener's, is to meet their needs as best we can: to give proper nourishment, love, attention, and caring, and to hope for the best.

—Katharine Kersey

Balance

In previous chapters we touched upon the damage school practices impose on children and, in the bigger picture, impose on society by attending only to intellectual development while ignoring other basic, human needs. One of schooling's saddest and most costly blunders, both in personal happiness and human potential, this imbalance can be avoided (or corrected) in the comfort of your home.

You put your family freedom and gift of time to their best use here. No longer caught up in schedules that leave you and your children passing each other's lives like ships in the night, you insure an education that includes attention to body, mind, and spirit. These terms, I'm sure, mean different things to different people. It doesn't matter. As long as you don't go overboard and merely create imbalance in a different direction (replacing intense focus on intellect with intense focus on religion, for example), your child will realize the balance, the wholeness, that is his birthright.

What, I hear you asking, will this do for my child? A child out of kilter feels an emptiness he is compelled to try to fill any way he can. Lacking life experience or reasonable alternatives, his methods of filling the emptiness often don't reflect much wisdom. This can lead to trouble, trouble that develops simply because he is not fulfilled. Like an empty river bed, there is no life-sustaining connection to replenishing sources.

On the other hand, a child educated with balance, or wholeness, is fulfilled. Like a healthy, running river, he is nourished by healthy tributaries; he flows smoothly along his course to eventual connection with a vast ocean. He finds union with his world.

> He knows that his own happiness comes from within, and therefore does not waste his life pursuing things which he has always possessed, such as happiness, love, success, and fulfillment. He brings these qualities to his life, rather than asking them from life.
> —Dr. Wayne W. Dyer in *What Do You Really Want for Your Children?*

A child with this truth-filled perspective brings a crucial understanding to everything he does. He knows life is meant to be lived. And in the singular act of living life to its fullest, in appreciating every moment as it unfolds, true education occurs. This is not to say that family centered educators remain in this state every minute of every day—nobody's perfect! But a child who grows knowing he already has inside that which others spend lifetimes searching for is building a life and an education on a strong foundation. The happiness, love, success and fulfillment he knows are inside shine forth in play, work, busy time, quiet time, triumphs and failures. Each action becomes its own reward.

> To find and appreciate beauty in the ordinary and the extraordinary is the right of every child for esthetic experience is a basic need of all men in their universal struggle to add meaning to life. We owe to children the freedom to explore the full range of their senses; to appreciate subtle differences; to be aware of beauty wherever it is found; to see, to touch, to smell, to hear, to taste, so that each in his own way will strive to find and express the meaning of man and human destiny.
>
> —From *Living & Learning: A Report of the*
> *Provincial Committee on Aims and Objectives of Education*
> *in the Schools of Ontario*, Ontario, Canada Dept. of Education, 1968

Common Sense

An important universal life skill emerging in many home-schooled kids' lives is good ol' fashioned common sense. Because your child will spend less time looking for external approval among peers (her positive affirmation comes from within), she'll look at common habits related to approval-seeking (alcohol and other drugs, sex, gangs, violence, etc.) with the total perception of all her senses, or what we normally call common sense. With total perception and wholeness, the typical "empty child" habits appear unattractive and unnecessary.

Unnecessary, too, are lots of videos, books, multi-billion dollar, tax-funded programs, and moralistic lectures on the dangers of negative behavior. Healthy, life-affirming behavior occurs, not because your child has been conditioned through fear or threat or indoctrination from a friendly policeman or priest or teacher, but because common sense prevails. The necessary "lessons" emerge from the place where balance has allowed happiness, love, success and fulfillment to spring forth.

Any additional information your child needs on drugs, AIDS, sex, etc. is easily transmitted by you through informal conversation and discussion. (Remember you are communicating in a new, improved relationship now.) Simply watching the news, reading newspaper and magazine articles, or viewing thoughtful movies about these topics with your child provides the opportunity for her to formulate questions and receive necessary information at the same time she becomes familiar with cause and effect, the best lesson inherent in so-called negative behavior. She develops common sense which will guide her well.

Free of the Degrading Grading Experience

OK, it's bad enough that school's myopic attention to the intellect creates damaging imbalance. But they add insult to injury when they place an extraneous value on your child's work; a value which routinely considers only the end instead of the means; a value increasingly questioned within and without the education bureaucracy. It all begins when she is assigned a slot, like all the children her age, in a grade level. Whose bright idea was this, anyway?

> A number of educators, impressed with the graded schools they had seen in Germany, had been proposing adoption of the technique in this country...With public school attendance mushrooming, the graded school was an important advance. It gave schoolmen a means of sorting and classifying the hordes of children pouring into the schools, along with a way of subdividing the knowledge to be taught.
>
> —Charles Silberman in *Crisis in the Classroom*

As the business of school really started booming in the mid-1800's, these schoolmen felt a need to sort and classify children. *Their* needs also dictated a subdivision of knowledge. They did this to fix *their* problems, not the kids'. I doubt they gave much thought to the legacy of learning-interference they set in motion at the same time. And since age grading soon wouldn't be enough, the children's performance would need to be judged and graded as well.

> The evidence strongly suggests that tighter standards, additional testing, tougher grading, or more incentives will do more harm than good.
> —Alfie Kohn in *Punished by Rewards*

Grade levels and grading, obviously, have much to do with running an institution and nothing to do with true education. Since you won't deal with "hordes" of children and the associated problems of managing them, there's absolutely no reason to impose these contraindicated practices on your own children.

Here are just some of the benefits your child will experience when unshackled from the degrading grading experience:

1) *Freedom from stress*—Researchers report symptoms of stress increasing even among kindergarten children. Working for grades under constant surveillance creates stress, and stress blocks clear thinking. Without clear thinking, good grades move that much further out of reach. It's a vicious cycle, one that *can* be broken when you remove the source of stress—working for a grade—and replace it with the knowledge that learning is natural and rewarding.

Home educators everywhere find that without the constant threat of "failure," there's actually a lot more room for success.

2) *Increased self-esteem*—In school, mistakes are devastating events resulting in anything from an "F" on a report card to abusive teasing from peers to the shame of public exposure. Your child need not fear these negative results when attempts at something new result in mistakes. In the warmer, more open home environment, she is naturally more inclined to experiment, which stretches and strengthens her abilities. Sure, she'll still make mistakes, but they are positive experiences, opportunities to learn. Your child knows she can try again—and again and again, if necessary. Self-esteem grows right along with your child, rendering separate "I Am Wonderful" classes superfluous.

3) *Freedom from competition*—No one has critically analyzed the harmful effects of competition in America's culture as thoroughly as Alfie Kohn in *No Contest: The Case Against Competition*. Please read this book for a clear picture of what competition in general, and school competition in particular, can do to your child.

Your child can eliminate competitive conditioning from his life and instead experience the fine art of cooperation and its rewards. It is not human nature to be competitive (as many "uncivilized" societies illustrate), despite our conditioning to the contrary. Life's most rewarding work practices, whether your child becomes a store clerk or an astronaut, involve cooperating with fellow workers (young and old). Letting your youngsters skip one year, two years, or twelve years of competition with classmates for grades and teacher attention puts them on track toward cooperation.

4) *Freedom from burn-out*—Early, formal learning attempted before a child is physiologically ready is a prescription for disaster. Researchers have linked our haste to train kids academically to vision and hearing problems, as well as socioemotional problems. Our accepted education practices greatly interfere with the brain's natural development, creating many of the learning problems schools then turn around and "fix" for us.

But early, institutionalized schooling also leads to a child burnt-out on learning, on Self, and on the greater community that fails him.

Read some of Dr. Raymond Moore's work for easy access to a universe of research contraindicating our accepted practices, particularly important as our nation daily moves dangerously closer to making those practices even worse. And if the findings of many researchers don't convince you of the reality of burn-out, perhaps what you already know in your heart will.

Mother Nature doesn't consult the school calendar as your child grows. Nature would no more force your child to be exactly three and a half feet tall by five years of age than urge all oak trees to rise to the same height. And if every lilac bush isn't obligated to bloom by April 30th, it's ludicrous to demand every child reads by grade one, eighth month.

As your child's most important, natural teacher, you are not compelled to force your child's blossoming. You possess the gift of time. Your child grows in understanding at his own pace following nature's schedule, not the school's. Learning is not a strain on as-yet-underdeveloped minds and bodies. Remember, when allowed, "Brains—and the organisms attached to them—tend to gravitate to the types of stimulation that they need at different stages of development."

Your child does not suffer "burn out" because learning is a drag. On the contrary. learning becomes his experience of life. Learning and life are one and the same, an experience too enjoyable to be a source of pain or displeasure or stress.

Your heart knows nature's way. So does your child. And, thank goodness, nature's way is not to evaluate, but to elevate.

Individual Interests, or the Pursuit of Happiness

The parents know that the child cannot be artificially motivated to learn; they know that he is already motivated by the strongest driving force on earth: his inner intent.

—Joseph Chilton Pearce in *Magical Child*

As a child, did you ever have to give up a practice that meant a lot to you? Maybe it was drum playing, or cave exploring, or baking sinfully rich desserts. Have you ever wondered what life may have been like had you continued this practice? Fuller, more meaningful, perhaps? Sorry. Like many of us, you may never know.

Your child doesn't ever have to wonder. She has time to explore interests to her heart's content. If those interests lead her to fulfillment and meaning, thank goodness nothing else forces her to turn her back on them. And there's no reason those deep, abiding interests can't become the centerpiece of her education.

Said another way, pursuing those interests can help her learn how to learn. Every interest carries a rich history, every interest incorporates a body of knowledge necessary to its practice. Many interests lead to other interests. Furthermore, asking our children to know something about everything in this Information Age is, as today's schoolmen admit, impossible.

You can subject your child to school's shot-gun approach to information (lots of rapidly-fired, scattered tidbits, chosen by bureaucrats in political ivory towers). Or, by learning at home, your child can employ an archer's approach: One arrow, purposefully chosen by the archer, and well aimed at a meaningful target. He opens wide the door to self-initiated learning based on individual interest. Your child dodges stress and failure and hits meaning and success. Best of all, he acquires another universal life skill. He learns how to learn, and applies this skill in myriad situations throughout his joyful learning journey.

Is a Hare Better than a Tortoise, or Just Moving at a Different Pace?

All children are not created alike. One flies through math books, easily grasping mathematical concepts and applying them to a pageful of problems before her. Another grasps math more slowly, but loves moving, with a ballerina's grace, on a ball field or in a gymnasium. Yet another finds math *and* movement difficult, preferring, instead, to surround herself with sound; music on recordings, learning and performing with an instrument, singing her questions aloud.

None of these children is necessarily "smarter" than the other. Each illustrates just one of seven different types of intelligence Harvard University Professor Howard Gardner discusses in *Frames of Mind*, a book outlining his theory of multiple intelligences. While everyone has his unique blend of all seven, one or a few dominate in individuals.

The seven types of intelligence are:
- Linguistic
- Logical-Mathematical
- Spatial
- Bodily-Kinesthetic
- Interpersonal
- Intrapersonal
- Musical

Unfortunately, schools concentrate on only two areas of intelligence; the linguistic and logical-mathematical. The child mentioned above who tears through math books will likely garner high grades and teacher approval in school. The other two children, equally intelligent in their own way, however, likely find their particular talents useless and unappreciated in the classroom. They won't even bother looking for their names on the honor roll. And in all too many cases, their particular talents wither and die from lack of use.

Home educated kids, pursuing individual interests, frequently do so while exercising their strong points, or their particular intelligences. And with freedom from a rigid curriculum, they move through their experience at their own pace. That means our example child, the math whiz, can move steadily along, taking his study to heights unknown. He won't be slowed down by a class moving at a rate suitable to tortoises when he is, in fact, a hare.

Our bodily-kinesthetic learner (the one who'd rather be running laps around the track than ciphering) won't be rushed in math class, either! The hare's pace could be too much for this type of learner. At home, he's free to be a math tortoise, taking his time and possibly applying learning alternatives which, for one reason or another, aren't allowed in the classroom. For example, sitting still and trying to memorize the times tables are sheer torture for this fellow. Instead he marches around the room counting rhythmically, clapping once on the multiples of two, then the multiples of three, and so on. It's too much noise for a classroom, but just fine in a living room.

Moving at one's own pace—following our innate tortoise or hare rhythm—greatly contributes to that sense of balance we all need. Adults don't like being told to work at a pace that either bores us or, at the other end of the spectrum, moves success beyond our grasp. Yet we ask this of our children every time we require them to perform according to an externally-dictated timetable that, for many, holds no rhyme or reason.

Doesn't it make sense to embark on the education journey from the best possible starting point, moving not too quickly nor slowly, but at a pace that gives us the best chance for a rewarding trip? Hares and tortoises exist side by side, each perfect in its own way, moving through life at the rate that best suits their survival. Your children can find the pace that best suits them, too, if you but free them to discover it.

The Animal School
By R. H. Reeves, Educator

Once upon a time, the animals decided they must do something heroic to meet the problems of a "New World," so they organized a school. They adopted an activity curriculum consisting of running, climbing, swimming, and flying. To make it easier to administer, all animals took all subjects.

The duck was excellent in swimming, better in fact than his instructor, and made excellent grades in flying, but he was very poor in running. Since he was low in running he had to stay after school and also drop swimming to practice running. This was kept up until his webbed feet were badly worn, and he was only average in swimming. But average was acceptable in school, so nobody worried about that except the duck.

The rabbit started at the top of the class in running but had a nervous breakdown because of so much makeup in swimming.

The squirrel was excellent in climbing until he developed frustrations in the flying class where his teacher made him start from the ground up instead of from the tree-top down. He also developed charley horses from over-exertion, and he got a "C" in climbing and a "D" in running.

The eagle was a problem child and had to be disciplined severely. In climbing class he beat all the others to the top of the tree but insisted on using his own way of getting there.

At the end of the year, an abnormal eel that could swim exceedingly well and could also run, climb and fly a little had the highest average and was valedictorian.

The prairie dogs stayed out of school and fought the tax levy, because the administration would not add digging and burrowing to the curriculum. They apprenticed their children to the badger and later joined the groundhogs and gophers to start a successful private school.

Take Good Care of Yourself!

When your child is free to be herself—to follow her fascinations in the most personally meaningful ways possible at a comfortable pace—she finds two more universal life skills: self-discipline and self-responsibility.

No longer driven by external means (grades, competition, fear, threat, reward, etc.), she feels the first stirrings of internal motivation. "I'm doing this because I *want* to," she thinks as she finishes the three hundred page novel, or returns home tired from a day visiting a local nursing home. "I think I'll try another book by the same author; I like her style," the student decides. "I'll bake some zucchini bread for Mr. Jones and take pictures of the play to share with Mrs. Smith when I go back to visit my seasoned friends."

Your child gets inspired with her own ideas. Your child follows through. No one need remind her to go to the library to get the novel *or* to have the bread and pictures ready on time. She handles the deeds because they are important to her. She accepts responsibility for accomplishment and provides her own, necessary discipline. Is this any way to run a life? You bet it is!

Qualities for Learning

With your guidance your youngster is learning life's most important lessons naturally—painlessly—carrying them always in his heart as well as his head.

But your child also brings much to the learning experience. These are the qualities of curiosity, imagination, creativity, inner peace, humor, artistry, self-motivation, and intuition, the qualities essential to true education.

These are the qualities we admire (and, go on, admit it, we also envy) in our culture's artists. Without the interference of school schedules, school focus, and school thinking, your child need not ever lose these qualities. She will apply her artistic skills to whatever work lies ahead in life, whether that's turning pirouettes center stage or pumping septic systems in the middle of nowhere.

Looked at another way, as your child grows she can use these qualities in all areas of life during all moments of life, thus transforming each activity into learning, wherever she happens to be, whatever she happens to do, with whomever she happens to do it. (The *real* world critics claim is missing from a homeschooler's life *is* her very "teacher.") Think of the possibilities for the greater community when more and more members of the human family bring these positive qualities into play.   (Important note: We'll visit those possibilities soon!)

All children need time to exercise their inherent characteristics if they are to grow and thrive. When you take responsibility for your child's education, you can make sure a lot of sun shines on these qualities. It's easier than you might imagine. In fact, kids do it naturally—through play. Is your child's natural impulse to play coincidence? Or simply "the way it's supposed to be?"

Relationships

> Bonding is a nonverbal form of psychological communication, an intuitive rapport that operates outside of or beyond ordinary rational, linear ways of thinking and perceiving.
> —Joseph Chilton Pearce in *Magical Child*

Interest-initiated education develops universal life skills, in part, because your child takes just one or a few interests at a time and dives as far to the depths of each as he can handle. The fine art of building relationships likewise thrives from a focused, in-depth experience.

Let's start from the premise that a child cannot love and respect others if he does not love and respect himself; he cannot bring forth what does not exist inside. With family centered education's attention to personally satisfying living and learning, your child grows receiving a steady supply of internally produced, positive affirmation. Consistently reinforced by *experience* and the warm, responsive home learning *environment*, he never loses love and respect of self.

Now he's got something—love and respect. Now he can spread it around! And he will. But consider this societal irony. We give young children a 5-piece puzzle before we throw 200 pieces at them. We let them write a sentence prior to requiring a paragraph. We figure, rightly so, that mastering the relatively simple addition must precede calculus. Yet when it comes to the "S" word—social-ization—we practice bigger is best. Our five year-olds (and, in many cases, two and three year-olds) must hobnob in a 200 piece social puzzle. Talk about your shock treatments!

If it makes sense to conquer the sentence first, if it makes sense to understand addition before calculus, it's not that great a leap of logic to conclude that, initially, a smaller socialization puzzle makes sense. The skills of cooperation (working as a team), along with etiquette, give-and-take, and polite conversation, are acquired more easily in the kitchen than on the playground. Here your child gets the time and attention necessary to master the smaller socialization puzzle, gradually moving on to more challenging encounters in the greater community as she acquires the skills and strength of nervous system to handle more pieces.

The slower, more gentle entry into the art of socialization gives your child a smaller field on which to shower his love and respect. All members of this more manageable field receive a nourishing amount which fills their cups. They may then shower more in return. This rewarding cycle becomes less and less likely as the size of the field the child is expected to cover increases. If the field grows too large prematurely, no recipient gets enough love and respect. They become such scarce commodities there is no love and respect to return, and the nurturing cycle screeches to a halt.

Our institutions still give lip service to the family as the first and most important building block of society. But by destroying the natural cycle of love and respect inherent in family life through their demands that children "socialize" in artificially inflated institutional settings, they are contributing to the destruction of society itself.

Through family centered education, you and your children have the opportunity to broaden and crystallize a few relationships, the ones that strengthen family. This includes the relationship between parents, between parents and child, and relationship among siblings. Now, don't get me wrong. Staying at home is not a miracle cure-all for sibling squabbles. (Sorry.) But you'll likely find that the frequency and intensity of disagreements decline as brothers and sisters, living a lifestyle that allows them to have more in common, get to know one another better and build mutual love and respect.

Relationships also extend beyond other people to the more encompassing aspect of traditions, customs, and history. America has always enjoyed a rich heritage of diverse cultures, but doesn't celebrate them on a level playing field. Our education institution has, of late, made strides in this direction but, once again, in a meaningless manner.

The contributions and customs of ethnic groups are being compartmentalized, tacked on to the rigid schedule. There they stay; supposedly equal, definitely separate. (Black History Month and Women's History Month are examples of this treatment.)

Even national holidays, like Lincoln's and Washington's birthdays, Memorial Day and Columbus Day, are no longer celebrated on the proper days. They mark, instead, three-day weekends for government employees. This was a government policy change which, through government's pervasive control of Americans' lives, dictates much of the American families' behavior, even down to when we plan vacations, parties, visits, and surgery. (Let's have everyone travel the country's highways and skyways at the same time—sound like a prescription for problems?)

With dozens of religions represented amongst the United States population, the school calendar remains centered around Christian holidays. The school doors close for Christmas and Easter whether you're Jewish, Hindu, Muslim, Native American or agnostic. Conversely, the school doors do open and your child is expected to attend even if it happens to be a non-Christian holiday important to you and your family.

Your children can utilize family centered education's freedom to integrate any and all celebration that holds personal significance. This includes customs and traditions school schedules force you to forego in the name of compulsory attendance laws. Conversely, if you desire, you can "school" right through Christmas and Easter, taking vacation at a time more appropriate to your heritage. You don't have to participate in three-day weekend traffic jams, either!

Of course you realize that when learning and life are one, you've less need for "vacation" as celebrations fit the family's rhythm like a hand in a glove. Following your hearts and souls instead of a school schedule, your relationship to that which has gone before—that which has helped shape you and influenced your environment and your thinking—becomes knowable. What a valuable contribution to an education that recognizes knowledge of one's Self as essential.

Relationships are too integral a link in the chain of human lives to be tampered with. Time and time again home educators acknowledge preservation of their family relationship as a most important benefit of their educational choice. Here is an example from a letter I recently received:

> I want to thank you for the article you wrote...several years ago. When I came across it for the second time (I had saved it, just in case) our public school experiences had deteriorated to the point where my husband and I said, "If other parents are out there teaching their kids, so can we."
>
> Three years after that turning point we are a closer, happier family. Homeschooling is a better way of life. Thanks again!

Homeschoolers are not ignoring the "socialization" problem. They are solving it. They have rediscovered the key to social relationships: Build them one step at a time. Your family is your child's 5-piece puzzle; her single sentence; her addition basics.

Isn't Mother Nature smart?

No Robots Here

Not too very long ago a book called *Do What You Love, The Money Will Follow* captured the media's attention. Its author correctly gauged that too many of us spend the majority of our lives pursuing careers or jobs for countless reasons totally unrelated to personal happiness or fulfillment. The book sold well because it struck a chord deep in the hearts of many who sensed there could be another way to put food on the table *and* live lifestyles that suit their inner needs.

If, by learning at home, your child grows without a daily dose of being taught, in Illich's words, "the need to be taught" and "indoctrination in accepted ideas," your child can save years of stress, disappointment and heartache by entering the work world with clear, personally meaningful goals.

Instead of being stripped of individuality through daily conditioning into a socially acceptable sameness, your youngster continues enjoying the freedom of being who he is. It's not that he's free to roam the streets or rob banks or play video games all day, as some homeschool critics either state or imply. Rather, his freedom to be himself without fitting into anybody's preconceived notion of what that's *supposed* to be (and on the school agenda, that's the same as everybody else!), brings meaning and joy to education. There will be no robots here!

Think of what this means in terms of economic freedom in your child's future. He doesn't have to be a consumer creature *if he chooses not to*. This truly opens a world of choice in terms of lifestyles he may pursue. While everyone needs a source of income, your child's thinking expands beyond the doctor/lawyer/truck driver choices toward which school conditioning aims him. This doctor/lawyer/truck driver mindset often leads to a lifetime ticket on the economic merry-go-round, not to mention the surrender of time and energy to external forces over which he will have little control.

If, as he grows and learns, your child realizes there exist better ways to spend his adult years, you will not have created yet another mindless consumer who, without thinking, cashes in his freedom for a few creature comforts. His life course can reflect, instead, understanding of a more gentle, natural way to tread upon his planet.

He understands himself well enough to evaluate his disposition toward any particular employment pursuit. He can comprehend the impact of economic decisions on his preferred way of life. He uses a much broader yardstick by which to measure success.

And he just may approach his life's work as art, just as you helped him do with this life journey called education.

You, as parent, are the *only* one who can set progress in motion for your child. There may be other ways to accomplish it, but you can start today, this very moment, if you choose to do it yourself through family centered education.

As these beneficial changes occur in our families' lives, it's not a huge jump to see that your community would experience change, too. Let's take a look at this community as the number of family centered educators increases and moves about freely in the greater world. You just have to remember we're talking about kids and families free of school schedules, free of a false view of education and learning, free to inquire at will, and free to pursue life, liberty and happiness, wherever that leads them.

CHAPTER FOURTEEN

BENEFITS FOR YOUR COMMUNITY

IT TAKES A VILLAGE TO RAISE A CHILD

Our children are not going to be just "our children"—they are going to be other people's husbands and wives and the parents of our grandchildren. —Mary S. Calderone

A s families restore balance to their lives, as these individual building blocks of society reclaim their right and thus the ability to learn and do what is best for their own children, suddenly we are building communities with the finest materials. Individual blocks are not kept under constant stress, nor are they created by a scientifically programmed machine built to stamp out carbon copies according to a mass-manufacturer's specifications.

No, folks. These new, improved building blocks of society are fashioned by hand, created by artists who bring great care and devotion to their work. These artists pay attention to detail, and they maintain a constantly evolving knowledge of their practice. The societal building blocks these artists create are much stronger—and happier.

Strong, happy building blocks form the foundation of strong, happy communities. Strong, happy communities nurture families, and a beneficial cycle of give and take restores meaning to all members' lives.

Your community houses people with many different backgrounds, from all walks of life, who possess a wide range of interesting, useful, specialized knowledge. From retirees to working folks, from the farm to the skyscraper, from the hobby painter next door to the retired fish and game warden across town, your neighbors are people who have, for years, gathered experience and information. They have not studied how to administer programmed instruction in college to be called teachers, so our expert-worshipping minds don't think of them as teachers in a broader sense of the word; yet they are the ones who spend their lives practicing what they know.

Homeschoolers know the rewards for children and communities when education is guided by practitioners instead of preachers. Sometimes a friendly visit ignites your child's imagination and she embraces a new interest with enthusiasm she "catches" from her neighbor. Oftentimes she gathers additional fuel for a fire already burning brightly. She may exchange "lessons" with her neighbor as they discover they have more in common than originally thought. And, along the path, she could "learn" her way into a job, possibly one created just for her. Always, her involvement moves her forward to new experiences and friends.

Knowledgeable, sharing adults make very good friends. And each is a thread linking your child to the greater community, acquainting her with the ways of the "real" world. Your child and her friend have many discussions about politics and personal history and the price of eggs during their time together. Each conversation provides a manageable glimpse into the concerns of adults who move about in the "real" world. Adults who, incidentally, hold perspectives on life that may be quite different than yours. With these community members your child exchanges ideas, asks why, explains why, debates, accepts or rejects, and reaches deeper levels of understanding of her world and the people in it, all without the worry of grades, tests, or the stigma of failure. Rather than sitting still for six hours a day being told what are right answers, the community itself provides your youngster the opportunity to discover enough about the world to *experience* the right answers directly, without watered-down textbooks or "politically correct" curricula perverting reality. Sadly, this direct experience is not available to kids compelled to attend an institution where the powers-that-be limit their socialization to same-age peers.

Headline: "Across the Board School Tax Cut; Lowest Rate Since 1965 When Unionization of Teachers Became Widespread"

If you ask at this point, "Why don't our schools change?" you open up the Pandora's box of American education. The answer to this question explains why the government could never *allow* the educational system to undergo the reform they incessantly shout about but will never accomplish, reform that is the vital prerequisite to improvement.

In a nutshell, "the system" won't change because education is a business so vast and wealthy, so politically useful and powerful, that it has become a linchpin of the economic and political status quo. The very schools Thomas Jefferson foresaw insuring individual freedom through free inquiry are systematically putting the people to sleep, negating any possibility of freedom. Change school—deal with an *awakened* populace—and you must be ready to give up what currently exists. Those who now wield the political and financial power control what exists, and they won't be ready to give it up anytime soon.

I doubt there's a community in America that wouldn't benefit if its school budget allowed a reduction in school taxes. Whether that "extra" money remains in the pockets of seasoned citizens to supplement their small, fixed incomes, or whether it helps the community in other directions, it could be more wisely dispersed. This could take the form of everything from improved or additional community services to not-quite-so-strapped parents providing healthier breakfasts to children with the "found" money.

It wouldn't even be so bad if success, even by the false definition, was the rule. But it's an increasingly rare exception. Remember that June 7, 1993 *Forbes* article referred to in "Running Into Walls?" It stated: "The [National Education Association's] rise is directly linked with the 30-year decline of American education that occurred simultaneously—not just in terms of quality, but especially in terms of quantity: education's crushing, and incessantly accumulating, cost."

Education's spiraling and ridiculous price tag is concurrent with the unionization of public sector employees. Very few can any longer say, at least without crossing their fingers behind their backs, that we're getting our money's worth.

There's a lot of talk about how the education system *is* failing. This implies it still has a chance to pass. It does not. The system has *failed*. It drains communities' resources, both monetary and human. It's easier to recognize the cost in terms of money. But communities also lose when they consider useless the talents and wisdom of so many residents whose spirits would soar if their neighbors acknowledged and benefited from their abilities.

There's growing scientific proof that people who feel connected to others are healthier. "Involvement in life helps prolong it," says a May 9, 1994 *Newsweek* article titled "The Death of a Spouse:

Mortality, says Duke University psychiatrist Daniel Blazer, is higher in older people without a good social-support system, who don't feel they're part of a group or a family, that they 'fit in' somewhere.

The article advises that the loved ones of a person recently widowed "can make sure that he or she is socializing, getting proper nutrition and medical care, expressing emotion—and, above all, feeling needed and appreciated." Needed, appreciated people are healthier. Healthier people create healthier communities.

Ignoring this human need for connection is the less visible yet more costly of the prices we pay for supporting schools. Wasting our neighbors' talent and wisdom keeps alive the myths that 1) only teachers can teach and 2) everyone needs a teacher to learn something. It's a lose-lose situation for the entire community.

It takes a village to raise a child is not just a cute saying or a punchy title for a social service seminar. It contains a universal truth about the human need for connection that transcends age— as well as religion, race, and nationality. Family centered educators have rediscovered the importance of connection to community as part of a child's education, a basic aspect of acquiring universal life skills as Ben Franklin, Abraham Lincoln, William Penn, and Winston Churchill did (for more "homeschooled alumni" see the appendix). This truth is that real learning occurs through the experience of connection—first to family, then to the greater community. Real education takes place in the real world. We, the people, have to *allow* the village to raise the child.

Homeschoolers aren't, as yet, reducing the staggering school taxes, but they sure are reducing waste of *human* resources as apprenticeships and mentorships spring up across the country. The village *can* raise the child when the child grows free of the institution's burdensome schedule.

(Author's note: Many mistakenly believe that the community is raising the child when it offers him all manner and form of "social services." These are merely more institutional surrogates stepping in to do what the family and community should and would accomplish if free to do so.)

Volunteer Corps Par Excellence

> We may discover that the best thing we will ever do for our families, however we define them, is to get involved in community or political action to help others.
> — Stephanie Coontz

A decrease in the financial burden of a dead institution, then, is not the only benefit the community would realize. Along with apprenticeships, many homeschooled kids expand their involvement in the community in a volunteer capacity. Volunteerism is one of the last ready-made forms of apprenticeship available today. Many volunteer organizations welcome the help of children, even if they're younger than "working paper" age.

Community service is a cornerstone of many homeschooling families' education. Your youngster might begin volunteering by your side at the community library, quickly growing into independent responsibilities. Animal shelter operators appreciate an extra heart or two, for when administrative duties are complete, there's little time left to personally attend to their charges. Young children can spend an hour or an afternoon combing, walking, playing with and petting puppies and kittens who appreciate the attention.

Think of all the services and organizations that could better serve your community if they had more hands and hearts to help. I guarantee you *somewhere* homeschooled kids are there. And the benefits naturally trickle out into the greater community, no matter how small that trickle may be.

President Clinton has recognized the value of community service but, alas, even something as rewarding as this can and will be adulterated in the wrong hands. "There is another element of Goals 2000 [the national education law] that should concern all parents," warns columnist Cal Thomas. "It is a mandate that 'all' students 'will' be involved in community-service activities. That's a civilian version of the military draft, but with no deferments."[1]

> *Soon-to-be-high-school-graduates receive their assignments and go out into the community for Senior Work Week. Two girls find themselves appointed to the Humane Society. Their lack of experience means limited knowledge and ability, so duties include walking the dogs, changing kitty litters, and cleaning canine cages.*
>
> *The more experienced, young volunteer is used to guiding neophytes through their duties. She demonstrates litter change for the Senior Workers, and gently urges them to proceed.*
>
> *"I'm not going to touch that," says one.*
>
> *"I can't believe we have to be here for a whole week," says the other.*

"Well," says the first, *"at least we didn't have to go to the old folks' home."*

Nothing will turn kids off to the value of volunteer work quicker than telling them they *have to do it* as part of school work. Their experience with school work is that it is boring and irrelevant. The kids can't help but carry this subconscious message over to additional school requirements. Through mandates, this rich life experience will become yet another compartmentalized, out-of-context, graded activity performed under duress—an obligation tacked onto an already too long list of others.

Kids who realize they are valuable family members *and* community members spend the journey toward adulthood experiencing and experimenting with self-confidence, responsibility, and compassion. As they know they are valued for real, meaningful contributions at home and in the neighborhood, so, too, do they value their homes and communities in return. It's hard to imagine that kids busily contributing to and receiving from the community could find the time or desire to destroy it. These could be the same kids now roaming around town looking for trouble who, free of daily institutionalization and false learning, enter the community complete with the qualities necessary for learning and the sense of connection necessary for self-responsibility. You may say I'm an idealist (or crazy!), but this approach to learning and life seems to be working in too many cases to be a false observation!

Could families teaching their own children reduce or eliminate the community's schools and their accompanying financial burden *and* initiate further expense reduction in the form of decreased vandalism, violence, crime, prisons, and psychologists? Could true volunteerism (contributing because they *want* to contribute) and apprenticeships bring the positive change to communities that schools, politicians, business, social programs, longer jail terms, more laws, and bigger police forces cannot? On a small scale, individual families are making it work. On a larger scale, more families could work miracles.

Any volunteers?

Learning Centers

Our communities are currently overrun by public school "educated" persons, many of whom "serve" their communities in their positions as government paid politicians. The political playing field has grown so large and specialized over the years that our schooled minds tell us the only ones who can run government today are those expert in it. But just as the rapid decline in school tests scores occurred simultaneously with unionization of federal employees and growth in spending, so, too, has the rapid degeneration of government and politics occurred simultaneously with our dependence on and, therefore, support of, political experts, or politicians, to manage our lives. A ridiculous growth in spending accompanied this, too.

The only way a community can reclaim itself is for its individual members to be educated, the way Jefferson meant education for the masses: an informed citizenry capable of governing *itself*. In other words, to be self-responsible. It is to everyone's benefit that this education be equally available to all, whether they are old or young, rich or poor, urban or rural, white, black, or purple.

After approximately twelve years in the institution we've been trained to think only in terms of public school for children roughly between the ages of five and seventeen or eighteen. But as long as we're broadening definitions, couldn't we think of the "public" in public school as *really* public? ("Maintained for and used by the people.") Those same twelve years in the institution taught us to confuse "school" with education ("to bring out that which is within). Couldn't we embrace education's true meaning and offer it to "the public?"

Laws currently compel school attendance (compel: "To gather or unite by force; to herd. From Latin *compellere,* "to drive [cattle] together." See synonyms at *force*). This very act flips education on its head. Instead of education guiding out that which is within (that which already exists), it becomes a matter akin to throwing equal amounts of Rice Krispies into all the empty boxes as they automatically pass by on a conveyor belt. Everyone needs to be herded together, united only by force.

What better gift could a community bestow upon itself than learning centers open to anyone and everyone *who wants to be there?* What better use of a community's resources, financial and human, than to take responsibility for itself? What better use of volunteer time to benefit all? If the community were able to build learning centers instead of prisons, were it able to shrink its police force instead of enlarging it, were it to reach a state of healthy self-dependence and require less government supervision and fewer government social agencies, that many more resources would become available.

Folks who like to garden use the community's public spaces as their hands-on laboratory for exploration (remove the cost of landscapers from the town tax budget). Folks who have found others interested in learning more about recycling further their study at the town's recycling center togethe. (the county needn't handle this any longer, remove cost from county tax budget). Those who attend the learning center's class on embroidery visit the nursing home each week, sometimes with their children or pets, honing their skills under the watchful eyes of true veterans (remove cost of depression medication from home's budget. Everyone seems to be feeling much better). And all, including teachers, are voluntarily gathered, not herded. All are united by common interest and purpose, not force.

In May, 1994, high school English teacher Craig Lancto wrote:

> There is no need for privatizing schools or dumbing-down the curriculum. I have a modest proposal to individualize instruction, shove home-schooling into the mainstream of society, save taxpayers money, improve teacher salaries, and significantly improve education and record-keeping.
>
> We can improve education and cut costs with one simple solution: Eliminate schools...I propose that we provide common rooms or lounges where students may gather to socialize and confer, discussing work or meeting each other.[2]

"Learning will thrive as schools change from institutions designed to force all into one amorphous package to open learning centers dedicated to meeting the unique needs of each individual learner and to challenging each to pursue unlimited learning," said Gene Lehman, former English teacher and creator of the Learning Unlimited Network of Oregon. "Learning will thrive as students, parents, teachers and the public take back personal responsibility for life and learning."[3]

When *Times Educational Supplement* reporter Virginia Makins investigated nearly 3000 children from over 300 English schools, their responses revealed an intuitive knowledge of what learning centers could be. "Our teacher makes me mad," confessed one child, "because she tells you to write a story and then after two pages she tells you to finish it even though you are in the middle."

These children wished for poetry, drama, and more time for reading and writing "so we can really let our imagination roll and finish with a good long story." At the end of the study Makins concluded: "The most extraordinary result...was the unanimity and conviction with which boys and girls aged 8-11 called for a broader curriculum, with much more science, geography, history, art, crafts, woodworking, electronics, cooking, and technology... They wanted, above all, more work which allowed them to think for themselves...They wanted to design and make things, to experiment, and to engage in first-hand observation."[4]

Simply by changing perspective, or thinking in terms of *really* public education, and stirring in a good mix of self-responsibility (seasoned with a wide variety of persons and abilities, of course), we change what we see when we envision places to learn. People come and go at will, whenever they find it necessary, all day long. They use computers to access information; they sit and read for a spell; they have meetings or classes or guest speakers; they pick up a video tape to watch that evening; they participate in art shows and craft sales, exhibits, and instruction.

You say this place sounds a lot like your community library? It does, doesn't it? Libraries are already in the learning center business, a ready-made guide to the change that must precede true education reform—if we choose *real* reform. Interestingly, as this notion of library as last bastion of free inquiry gains more and more recognition, libraries across the country see their piece of the tax-money pie steadily shrinking.

Listen to yet another teacher, John Taylor Gatto, speak of libraries:

> ...The library seems to have intuited that common human judgment is adequate to most learning decisions. The librarian doesn't tell me what to read, doesn't tell me the sequence of reading I have to follow, doesn't grade my reading... It doesn't send letters to my mother reporting on my library behavior... Everyone is mixed together there, and no private files exist detailing my past victories

and defeats as a patron... It is a very class-blind, talent-blind place, appropriately reflecting our historic political ideas in a way that puts schools to shame... you almost never see a kid behaving badly in a library or waving a gun there—even though bad kids have exactly the same access to libraries as good kids do.[5]

What would community learning centers look like? That's the fun part: they can be whatever the community wishes to create.

Jerry Mintz, alternative education advocate and publisher of the AERO-Gramme networking newsletter, shares a few examples. In a Paris, France suburb, families meet for half the day in different members' homes. Two people "teach," one makes lunch for the group, and the group only plans two weeks at a time. They've been at it for fifteen years. When asked what he likes best about his school, one "student" replied, "It is not a school."[6]

The Common Ground Community in Lexington, Virginia, meets three days a week. They've hired a resource person to work with members alongside volunteering parents.

Providence, Rhode Island is home to the Educational Resource Center of Rhode Island, serving more than thirty learning families. Community members offer classes for parents and children three and a half days a week.

Home educator Shara Spilker imagined convenient, low-cost learning opportunities for her three children, and founded what has grown into Kansas City's Franklin Learning Center. The center started with a once a week, six week schedule serving fifty families. As the center grew, it incorporated, needed and found a larger facility, accommodated one hundred families with more classes, and staged its first theater production. "The key to a successful learning cooperative is organization, and *lots* of volunteers," says Janie Cheaney, a creative writing teacher at the Center. "All interested parties must understand that everyone has to take a hand."[7]

Some learning centers serve families on a national basis through the mail, like Clonlara School in Ann Arbor, Michigan. Former public and parochial school teacher Pat Montgomery, Ph.D. aids homeschoolers in preparing curricula and choosing books. Clonlara provides full transcripts and a private school diploma (and graduation ceremony) to its graduates. They handle the administrative duties associated with home education, as well, and will act as a contact person between families and school administrators, if necessary.

Perhaps the most non-traditional learning centers today (although they're not called learning centers), are those without the usual four walls. These centers are held together, instead, by the hearts and hands of homeschooling families who donate countless hours to local, regional and state networking, drawing together those whose dedication to children's education leads them to create opportunities for all.

The New Mexico Family Educators (NMFE) is a good example. They publish a monthly newsletter called *The Connection*, a delightful potpourri of news and information. The latest issue contains names and phone numbers of contact people throughout the state, an ad for their summer "Talent Showcase," a used learning materials sale, art resources, a "Suggestion Box," reports on the NMFE Youth Conference, announcements for play groups, scouting, an outdoor club, a Catholic homeschool group meeting, free dental sealants for home-educated children at three locations, and the NMFE Library where members have access to books, magazines, and educational material catalogs for the asking. My favorite section is the "Kids' Korner" which highlights the children's writing and art work, as well as announcing the achievements of homeschooled kids.

The Massachusetts Home Learning Association's quarterly newsletter provides readers with news on conferences, courses, resources, camps, volunteer opportunities, and "Community Connections," a section where help and educational experience are asked for and offered. Reprints of important articles from homeschooling magazines and other state newsletters, as well as exclusive articles, round out their pages.

There are too many "wall-less" learning centers like these around the country to describe them all here. However, if you want to find out more about your region or state, simply contact some homeschoolers near you, and they'll likely be able to guide you straight to the information you're looking for.

One thing learning centers everywhere seem to hold in common is their flexibility. Their lack of multi-layered bureaucracies, coupled with continual input from participants, provides lots of growing room and the ability to serve the individual community's ever-expanding, ever-changing needs without undue delay.

Community learning centers can be large or small, well-funded or run on a shoestring. They can serve as a gathering point of community energy for the benefit of all its inhabitants. They can, in short, be whatever individuals in the community have the will and determination and commitment to create. Havens of education in its truest and purest sense, learning centers could be places where self-responsible citizens freely unite in bonds of purpose and mutual interest, leading us much closer to the art of education than today's education system will ever be able.

Tomorrow's Leaders

We know those who hold the power and the money in today's education system would fear reform that puts children's education ahead of profit, prestige, convenience, and employment security. But what do we, the people, have to be afraid of if government loosens its monopolistic grip on our time and our minds?

Are we afraid the kids would hang around in gangs? They already do. Are we afraid the kids will turn to crime and violence? The number who currently do so is far too high to say schooling is stopping them. Are we afraid the kids wouldn't show up at the learning center? 383,000 students dropped out of school in 1992. In case you think by virtue of your color or income you don't have to worry about this number, "the majority of students who dropped out over the last year were white, were under 20 years old, and lived in middle income families and in suburban or non-metropolitan areas."[8]

Should we fear the four year-olds who are not ready to go into school (of course they're not ready!)—or the 700,000 kids yearly coming out the door at the other end unable to read their diplomas? Should we fear an increase in teen substance abuse and pregnancy—or the fact that today 350,000 children are born each year to mothers addicted to cocaine during pregnancy, not to mention the children suffering Fetal Alcohol Syndrome? Should we fear kids who wouldn't receive public school's job preparation training—or the fact that since 1987, one out of four U.S. preschool kids is born into poverty?[9] Should we fear a few million parents staying home to nurture and educate their kids—or the two million children who today receive no adult supervision after school?

It seems there's already so much to fear about the way things are under current practices, families and communities couldn't make things worse if they tried! And when you've hit bottom, as long as you don't just keep doing more of the same, there's nothing to do *but* improve.

Where will tomorrow's honest, compassionate, innovative, inspiring leaders spring from? Will they emerge from the institutionalized herd? Or will they be the children who have been blessed with "1) much time spent with warm responsive parents and other adults, 2) very little time spent with peers, and 3) a great deal of free exploration under parental guidance?"[10]

If you're a betting person, put your money on the latter. It happens to be the "recipe" for high achievement as contained in the Smithsonian Report on genius. The study's director, Harold McCurdy, deduced: "The mass education of our public school system is, in its way, a vast experiment on reducing...all three factors to a minimum; accordingly, it should tend to suppress the occurrence of genius."[11]

I've never personally met a homeschooling family who is practicing the art to purposefully cultivate genius in their children (although I'm aware these families are around). A world-renowned genius in quantum physics or solar energy development would be a nice by-product of the homeschool experience. But a genius in caring for young children or lawn mower repair is much more practical and extremely likely to emerge in a family centered education environment. Again, let us deal with a broader definition of genius than we're used to.

Does someone like Einstein come to mind when you think genius? That happens if we think of genius as "exceptional or transcendent intellectual and creative power." But if we stretch our minds (and look a little further in the dictionary), we realize genius also means "a natural talent or inclination."

The natural talent or inclination of tomorrow's leaders in everything from politics to science to parenting to business to education to writers and other artists is best nurtured in freedom from an institution's compulsory attendance and a one-size-fits-all curriculum. Free exploration not only provides opportunity for a community's children to *discover* their natural talents, it also gives them a chance to *exercise* them. Warm, responsive parents and other adults provide the child with example and unconditional guidance. Very little time spent with peers increases time spent with the previously mentioned adults, and greatly decreases the child's chance of becoming blindly peer dependent.

From this perspective, the high achievement recipe looks natural, logical and, relatively speaking, quite inexpensive. And it's designed to be used by laymen—you and members of your community.

Tomorrow's world is shaped by the paths we offer our children today. The widely accepted, rarely questioned path of public schooling shows our children little hope for today, let alone tomorrow. The Smithsonian report indicates that the path to genius leads *away* from public schools *toward* home. Your community, and others just like it across the country, can provide essential support to those families who know it's time to go home. Communities are an essential ingredient in the genius recipe, for this is how family centered educators add flavor—more warm, responsive adults—to their children's high achievement souffle.

The community that today smoothes its members' path to genius will receive, in return, the guidance and leadership of tomorrow's young men and women who have freely developed their natural talents, at the same time getting to know and care about the people and concerns of their community.

The path to genius runs straight down Main Street, USA.

CHAPTER FIFTEEN

A DOZEN SIMPLE STARTING POINTS

Four years was enough of Harvard. I still had a lot to learn, but had been given the liberating notion that now I could teach myself.

—John Updike

Your child doesn't have to wait until college age to be "given the liberating notion" that she can teach herself. Your family can begin here and now—the very moment you lay this book down—on a learning journey that lets you claim again your children, your community, and your Self as your own.

You've learned about the rewards of true education, education in as artful and natural a state as you'll likely find anywhere, including the most expensive schools or programs and curriculum resulting from education "reform" laws. You've got lots more learning ahead of you—thinking, reading, thinking, talking, thinking, writing away for more information, and more thinking. More time, more work, more dedication, more courage, more trust. But you can get a running start with these dozen simple starting points that you can use immediately, whether your child is in school, out of school, preschool, elementary school, middle school, or high school.

You might say these ideas, gathered from my own experience and the experiences of other homeschoolers, can guide you to a different way of seeing life, learning, and your unique and important role in the lives of your children. For it is in seeing differently that you will lay the foundation for family centered education experiences in your home. Incorporate all or just a few of these starting points into your family's life, and you'll get a sense of the joy and freedom that await you.

Someone once said you don't have to be good to start, but you have to start to be good.

As always, it's your choice.

Simply Supply the Materials

When a carpenter builds, a seamstress sews, or an EMT rescues, day's end brings accomplishment she can see and touch. Not so with your child. After a day of family learning activities, your youngster is still the same size and his sneakers are still untied.

Some days you'll swear your time would be better spent peeling bananas for hungry jungle monkeys. A monkey with a full tummy at least represents immediate gratification and a sense of successful conclusion for your efforts.

In a society that measures success in tangible results (most frequently dollars!), it's difficult to gauge the value of any work that doesn't offer immediate, concrete rewards. The important aspects of education—self-respect, responsibility, compassion, and self-reliance, among others—can't easily be measured on a scale.

Your efforts may, at first, seem more like scrap lumber randomly scattered across the vast universe that is your child rather than a remarkable structure you watch rise, floor by measurable floor. But the Eiffel Tower didn't appear overnight, and the most beautiful cathedrals of the world took decades to complete.

It helps to think of yourself not as "teacher" the way you remember it, but like the supplier whose purpose is merely making sure the builder—your child—can get his hands on the necessary materials when he needs them. Be happy when you make any sale, however modest. The true architect will use the materials in his own way, in his own time.

Schools force a child into using his limited resources today. "Build a bird house," they demand, "so we may count how many sticks you've collected."

At home there's no need for immediate "proof." Be patient. Don't measure. Who can say what exquisite masterpiece your child will shape and build from the scraps tomorrow—or ten years from now? The more he collects, the greater the structure he's capable of building. And when that structure is life itself, don't settle for a bird house today. Trust you'll find a castle tomorrow.

Simply provide the materials.

Simply Visit Your Community

> The car trip can draw the family together as it was in the days before television when parents and children actually talked to each other.
>
> - Andrew H. Malcolm, *NY Times*

Your neighborhood houses folks with many interesting jobs and hobbies. Lots of them are ready and happy to share their enthusiasm and in-depth knowledge with youngsters eager to understand their world.

Only one business ever turned down my request for a tour, a local advertising agency I thought would tie in nicely when my kids and I learned about commercials and marketing. The agency claimed it was against their policy. The kids concluded that was not very good advertising, a terrific lesson without ever walking out the door!

Don't be afraid to ask for what you want. The worst thing that can happen is that someone says no, and most people don't. Call or write to schedule an appointment that's convenient for every-one. Remember your children's schedules, too: don't commit yourself at baby's nap time or when empty stomachs interfere with attention, energy and attitudes.

Don't ask your neighbor to take the time to commute to your home. Offer to do the traveling yourself. Not only is it more polite, there's a distinct advantage. Along with getting to know your neighbor, you'll get a feel for the workplace and see (and pos-sibly touch and use!) the tools, too.

Your neighborhood excursions also give your family socializa-tion opportunities traditional schools can't provide. Were your host neighbor to address a gymnasium teeming with kids, or even a classroom group of 20 to 30, a "talk" becomes remarkably simi-lar to a "speech." With your little group, though, you benefit from more intimate sharing, personalized attention, and the comfort of informality.

In a large group, a child feels lucky to get one of his questions answered. When my family ventures out on its own, we average at least ten questions apiece, even me! Informality breeds open-ness, and no one fears his question will be labeled stupid. No one worries that peers might criticize if he appears interested.

Ask your kids what they would like to know. What does an architect do all day? Why are there so many chemicals in a pho-tographer's dark room? How is the daily newspaper printed?

Find out. Simply visit your community.

Simply Press the "Off" Button...

...on the television set. Some folks suggest you put it in a closet or sell it at your next garage sale. A less radical approach, if you count on the tube for news and information, would be to make sure it's put only to positive use. After all, "TV has been linked," says author and learning specialist Thomas Armstrong, "to declines in test scores, decreased literacy, increased aggression, reduced play activity, drug and alcohol abuse, and even heightened cholesterol levels." Whether or not you've noticed one or all of these results in your child's life, you might want to learn a bit more about our technological wonder. Check the "Learn More About It" section for a few books that explore in greater detail how detrimental unlimited or unsupervised use of television has been for kids and the faculties they need to obtain a true education.

When you press the "off' button, you'll increase the time available to you as a family. Depending on how much TV they're used to consuming, your kids will need to be shown, by your example, alternative ways to spend their time. You can use this time for conversation, playing games, baking, reading, raising animals and plants, playing sports, journal writing, dancing, or a thousand other activities. It won't be easy at first; lots of people have a favorite show they can't imagine missing, and it may seem awkward trying to fill the void turning off the TV creates. But keep at it. The time you free will fill with meaningful interaction instead of passive, parallel existence where everyone is lost in a world designed to take your attention away from life.

There are ways to tame the pervasive influence TV holds over your family. *After* you've limited TV time, make a point of viewing chosen programs with your kids. Talk about what you see—everything from the reality of the main characters' circumstances and their reactions to them, to how the director uses the camera and music to control the viewer's mood and emotions. It's an important step in self-responsibility to know when and how one is being informed, entertained, or manipulated.

Ask questions like, "What would *you* do if you were him/her/them?" but be prepared for some interesting answers, and to temper some far-out misconceptions your child has of human strength, the capacity of automobiles, and the likelihood of a "bad guy" talking about his troubled childhood until the "good guys" arrive just in the nick of time. And don't be afraid to press the "off" button if a program looks like it's quickly going nowhere, no matter how much time you've already invested in it. Junk is junk no matter how it ends. You might better use the time having everyone create a finale together.

Your TV can, on the other hand, link your family to a wide array of culturally enriching experiences. While "live" is always better than recorded, you may not have an option to view performances in person if you live in a very rural area or if the price of tickets means you'd have to do without two weeks' worth of groceries. In that case, half a loaf of bread is better than none, and TV can deliver that half loaf.

You can view a ballet, listen to an opera, discover a symphony in Vienna, tour the world's finest art and history museums, or travel to Brazil, the Fiji Islands, and Australia's outback without having to pack. You can climb Mt. Everest or view the wreck of the Titanic without getting winded or wet. Why waste so much time watching actors get shot and cars blown up when for the same price of admission you can view just a bit of the world's immeasurable beauty?

Since today a TV without a VCR is like a cowboy without a horse, you've got even more access to specialized programs you can view at your convenience (or when your child's interest flairs). *Gone with the Wind* brings the Civil War to a human level, albeit a la Hollywood. The plight of pandas grows heartbreakingly real after sharing an hour with them via a *National Geographic* video. And I stuck *All the President's Men* into the VCR after my twentieth attempt to explain Watergate to my teen-aged son sounded more like doublespeak than U.S. history!

TV, then, may best be considered a tool, like a tablesaw. Used improperly and without safety guidelines, a tablesaw can ruin your life. Used appropriately with the guidance of a caring adult, a tablesaw is useful and productive. With your attention, your TV tool can supplement your family's knowledge of the world. Just remember that when you're done...

...simply press the "off" button.

Simply Be Quiet

If you needed to wrestle with life's greatest problems right now, would you run to Grand Central Station to figure them out? Not likely. You would probably seek out a comfortable, quiet place where enough time and space exist to put your thoughts and feelings in order.

Your child needs this type of quiet time, too, maybe even more than you do (think of how much he has yet to figure out). Yet society's intense concentration on false success and the constant motion necessary to "arrive" there makes it increasingly difficult to find this necessary stillness.

Quiet time offers the very best opportunity for your child to discover there is joy in tranquility. His nervous system receives a well-deserved break from the typical state of arousal and alertness constant activity requires. This pause permits him to maintain a balance of activity/rest necessary for good mental, physical, and spiritual health.

Quiet time provides a chance to dream, to stretch toward possibilities unlimited in his youthful imagination.

Quiet time furnishes opportunity for introspection, a most effective way for your child to understand Self. Through introspection he achieves a comfort zone in the inner world. He knows he is an important aspect of the outer world.

Quiet time encourages thinking. During peaceful moments free inquiry dives deeper and rises higher because stress does not block energy or movement. Quiet time also allows your child to put the new pieces into place when new ideas, discoveries, and sensory input fill the day.

If your child is used to lots of activity, start off slowly, maybe fifteen minutes before bedtime (remember the TV isn't on!). The two of you will discover when and how gradually increase and change should occur. Don't be afraid to experiment. And don't be surprised when your child claims additional time as his own—it means he knows he's found a treasure!

Simply be quiet.

Simply Do Nothing... Together

Maybe it's because the Information Age's frantic pace makes family time as difficult to find as it is loaded with responsibility. Or maybe it's because "experts" everywhere justified "quality" time as a replacement for plain ol' time when women were lured onto the economic merry-go-round. Whatever the cause, it's hard for many families to simply be together today.

If you work all week, weekends disappear in a blink of an eye as you "catch up" on chores, errands, and other important tasks that don't get accomplished Monday through Friday. So you feel that whatever time you do have "left over" should be devoted to "doing" something with or for the kids. (That inner urging to attend to the children is quite natural; it's the guilt and the self-incrimination that are unnatural, created by external forces.)

One of the healthiest, most loving things you can do for your children and your Self is to give them your attention, your time, your ear, your heart. "If a child is to keep alive his inborn sense of wonder," Rachel Carson wrote, "he needs the companionship of at least one adult who can share it, rediscovering with him the joy, excitement and mystery of the world we live in."

You can offer your child that ideal companionship by spending unscheduled, unshackled, unadulterated time together. It's perfectly fine to let simple activities creep in. Make popcorn, take a walk, paint rocks, or star gaze, as long as you can do it as a team—talking, laughing, sharing, dreaming together.

Just as quiet time benefits an individual, quiet time as family enhances you as a group, a whole. Bonding occurs, filling, as it should, the need all humans have to connect to others. And a child who fulfills this need at home doesn't need to go out and join gangs, engage in premature sex, or do something "wrong" in order to forge connection with peers who happen to be rebelling against the injustice they feel with confusion and anger and hate.

Remember the billboard that used to say, "The family who prays together stays together?" This thought, carried one step further, might read: "The family that *does* together, stays together." For a family "doing" together is not only physically united, but emotionally and spiritually united, as well. You get the chance to know your children as people; not three year-olds or sixth graders or learning disabled or gymnasts or even "the smart one" or "the bad one." Just as people, the way you know your friends. You learn "where their heads are at," what excites them, what bothers them, what they're afraid of, what they're proud of, how they perceive the world, how they perceive themselves, why they hope for what they hope for, why they dream the dreams they do.

This "knowing" is available to you and yours.
Simply do nothing...together.

Simply Talk About Education

Many families' communication about education is a variation of this:

"Hi. How was school today?"

"O.K."

That's it. (Alright. I suppose kids who witness a fight or a drug bust or a stabbing or who got stopped at the metal detector on the way into school might share their news—but I wouldn't bet on it.)

Kids trust other kids in large part because they don't trust adults. (I'm sure you remember this!) It's hard to share how a day in school *really* went with someone you don't trust with your true feelings. But the more time you spend together as family, the greater the trust; the greater the trust, the greater the truth shared. You'll find out what your youngster's perspective on education really is. You may find her picture reflects a lot of misconceptions (I go to school so I can get a good job someday.), misunderstandings (Good/bad grades mean I'm a smart/stupid person.), misgivings (I go to school because I *have* to), or mistakes (I have a right to be told what to do!). Share with her, to whatever degree her abilities allow, the true meaning of success, and the difference between education and conditioning. Allow her time to ponder this different perspective and to examine her own education, if her reasoning ability warrants this.

Try reading *The Education of Little Tree* by Forrest Carter together. This book will make you happy, sad, mad, and glad, for it's a really good read. But it's also a wonderful example of these "new" ideas applied to a Native American family's life long ago.

One more good way to get your finger on the pulse of public school life is by talking to other children. Each child's experience is unique, and each contributes to a clearer picture of the whole. Just one word of caution: Be ready to hear just about anything, and to become aware of situations you would like to change, but are unable to.

Simply talk about education.

Simply Touch Your Roots

Hug a tree...or sing to a flower or kiss a frog, just as long as you do it in the great outdoors!

Kids and nature go together like macaroni and cheese. They always seem to find lots to do in this place where "there's nothing to do," and the results usually bring forth that radiant glow of discovery on young faces. Even jaded teens have been known to fill with wonder at the sight of fresh bear tracks on the trail ahead, or a tiny fawn laying quietly where his mother protected him. Free of the distractions of everyday life—TVs, phones, neighbors, radios, school books—there's nothing else to do in the natural world *but* explore and create.

Contact with the earth—dirt, air, water, plants and creatures—serves a banquet to our senses and a drink to our souls. It fulfills an innate drive to connect to something beyond our immediate environment of concrete and steel and blacktop. Contact builds respect for our fellow earth residents, and broadens our perspectives as fauna shows there are many different ways to organize society for survival and growth, and flora proves life's greatest beauty resides in the abundantly simple. The entire experience is one of connection.

Perhaps Chief Seattle said it best in 1854 when he addressed the tribal assembly:

> This we know. The Earth does not belong to man; man belongs to the earth. Man did not weave the web of life, he is merely a strand in it. Whatever he does to the web, he does to himself. All things are connected like the blood which unites one family. All things are connected.

Children do not easily relinquish their link, though enough concrete and walls and climate controlled rooms will eventually blur it. So seek out opportunities to commune with the planet. A forest would be nice, but an empty lot, a city park, or a tiny backyard garden are natural wonderlands, too. The ocean would be fantastic, but a river, a pond, a swamp, or a puddle all hold their own mystery. An insect collection, a bat house, a bird feeder, a caterpillar, or a turtle egg invite your child to get to know different species "close up and personal."

Just remember before you do the laundry: The first place a nature collection starts is in the pockets!

Simply touch your roots.

Simply Watch the Dust Settle

You've just finished tonight's chapter of the family's bedtime book and tucked the last child into bed. As you descend the stairs your eyes scan the living room: There are three gaps on the bookshelf where the D, K, and S encyclopedias belong; tiny pieces of magazine and newspaper pages, along with the scissors and glue, are scattered across the floor (are those pieces on the coffee table glued into place?); the telescope lies inside the front door—barely; the desk drawers yawn back at you, still open from the mad search for paper clips.

The kitchen, you soon see, looks even worse.

Do you spend the rest of your evening vacuuming, wiping, and straightening up?

No. In the morning, every available pair of hands will help. (You may want to pick up the scissors!)

If you're a neat freak, the thought of having your kids creating and exploring in and around the house all day could lead you to scream, "Not me!" But you'd be thinking with your "old" mind again.

With few exceptions, home educators say they begin each day doing household chores—as a family. From cleaning up yesterday's mess to laundry to dusting to gardening to window washing, kids are capable of a lot more household responsibility than we normally allow them. But you'll have to lower your standards and settle for what I lovingly call "kid cleaned."

"Kid cleaned" means *some* of the laundry will be put in the right pile, *some* of the dust will be displaced by the cloth, and *some* of the library books will be readily found when you need them again. "Kid cleaned" means *most* of the dishes don't have egg on them, *most* of the rug will be visible after a vacuuming, and *most* of the garbage has found its mark. "Kid cleaned" means *all* do whatever they can to contribute, *all* realize they are part of a cooperative group effort, and *all* will, eventually, know how to do it *all*.

Granted, you will not likely invite *Good Housekeeping* photographers for a tour of the house and you *are* likely to apologize (frequently) to visitors for the inconvenience of having to sidestep the replica Roman Villa (complete with aqueducts) that graces your driveway.

For your sanity's sake, just think of your home as a learning laboratory where resident scientists conduct experiments in the field of life. As a science laboratory must, of necessity, stay cluttered with materials the scientists need so, too, does your home overflow with the tools of your children's very important trade called learning. When you consider your home as the location of a grand experiment in a better way of life, it's easier to look at the mess as a minor inconvenience that leads to major accomplishments.

Experiment #44: "We'll Have You Fix Your Own Dinner"

Oldest child resists. Middle child thinks it will be great fun. She heads straight for the biggest bowl in the house ready to create a salad for her and me. Suggested a smaller, "big" bowl. Oldest child thrilled when he learns he can make fried eggs. Squeezes two out of three yolks to oblivion while cracking. Upset with appearance, but he perseveres.

I prepare bacon and youngest decides to try yellow eggs (scrambled). Oldest child watches over these from his post in front of the stove. Middle child has most of the refrigerator contents scattered across the table for use in the salad. Before she can finish her masterpiece I stand helplessly, pot holders in hand, watching smoke billow out of the oven. The bacon is extra, extra crispy but served, nevertheless.

Fried egg yolks turn rubbery. Middle child drowns the salad in a whole bottle of Italian dressing. Youngest decides he doesn't like yellow eggs, but has two of everything else.

Results: Oldest child — "It's not the best, but it will do."

Middle child — "Next time I'll put in more lettuce and less dressing."

Youngest child — Tried something new.

Let the kids *use* the house. Let the kids *clean up* the house.

While their playmates sit and read books about self-responsibility and grow up thinking Mom is a synonym for maid, your kids live self-responsibility and realize Mom is but one of the team that is your family.

Simply watch the dust settle.

Simply Network

Everybody's doing it—networking, that is. And family centered educators across the country find it easier than ever to get in touch with like-minded folks via conferences, retreats, phone calls, travel directories, magazines, computers, books, and local, county, state, and national support groups.

When our family started learning at home just a decade ago, it was easier to get a Congressman to admit a political faux pas than it was to find information on homeschooling (and, as I recall, it was two words back then). Information obtained from my State Education Department was useless (though they didn't forget to inform the superintendent of our local school district that I had inquired about such things). But each piece of information from within the homeschooling community that I managed to get my hands on referred me to at least one more source. With determination, I eventually discovered all I needed to know. (With time, I eventually discovered I *already* knew all I needed to know.)

Today information on home education is as accessible as your local library, bookstore, or copy of *Home Education Magazine* on your newsstand. Better yet, community announcements in your newspaper or library can guide you to a local homeschooler's home for a support group meeting.

Support groups come in all shapes and sizes and meet different needs for different people. An initial phone call to a contact person can help you learn more about the group. If it sounds like it might be what you're looking for, attend a few meetings. New home educators can save lots of time and money and mistakes simply by asking questions of those who are already on the path. You'll find out about field trips, resource catalogs you've never heard of before, and the state regulations or laws that could affect your practice.

Practicing homeschoolers are also the best source of news and information regarding the climate for homeschooling in your school district. Many new home educators tend to overdo the paperwork they submit to authorities, fearing that if they accidentally leave something out somewhere the sky will fall and they'll be forever banished from learning at home. Those who have been through the mill before you can save you time if the bureaucratic requirements are less than you think. They can save you stress and worry, too, by guiding you through the bureaucratic maze if control and regulation are tighter than you thought.

The like-minded folks around you will provide inspiration when you've had a whole string of "one of those days." They can keep you from getting too serious about yourself, and point out exactly how much you *have* accomplished when accomplishments are hard for you to find. People who understand what you're doing provide a solid sounding board for your ideas and inspirations, basing feedback and criticism on experience.

He who gives the most gets the most, too, and no matter whether your family has homeschooled for one week or one decade, there's something *you* can do for your support group in return. Whether you arrange a field trip, type up a phone list, tack up meeting notices around town, or open your home for an afternoon craft fest, this is the stuff support groups thrive on. Support is a two-way street. So let those like-minded folks help as you lay your foundation, but make sure some of those blocks have your sweat on them, too.

Simply network.

Simply Love a Pet

In a home where family members disappear into the greater world for a large portion of each day, keeping a pet is a cruel notion for all involved. But if you've decided to test the family centered education waters, your new lifestyle can encompass the very best of caring for and loving a pet.

A family dog encourages long walks and more time spent in the woods, at the park, or strolling down the street saying hello to neighbors. He can discover water where you thought there was none (perhaps a great place to observe tadpoles), lead you to a brand new blueberry patch, or provide a real-life example of what happens when you don't watch where you're walking and disturb a hornet's nest!

If dogs aren't your idea of fun, there's also cats and rabbits and hamsters and snakes and ferrets and fish and guinea pigs and parakeets and goats and sheep and horses to choose from. And what do all these pets have in common?

Kids take responsibility for them. Now they stretch self-responsibility to responsibility for someone beyond themselves. Now the decisions of how to spend greater amounts of their time are rooted in greater responsibility ("Yes, I can spend the night, but I have to be back early to get the dog to the vet"). Successfully climbing larger steps of responsibility leads to acceptance of and ability for even more. Who has got time to hang around street corners or start fights when there's so many *important* things to do?

Caring for and about a pet will grow into caring for and about all the earth's creatures, both those with waggy little tails and those without. Allow your child the freedom to handle responsibility, and the perfume of compassion fills the air.

It should be obvious by now that kids don't learn anything by being lectured to about responsibility. They need the freedom to practice responsible behavior. With family centered education, you provide the perfect opportunity. Your kids take opportunity and run with it. A pet is just one of many ways you'll discover for adding responsibility to your child's growing list of universal life skills.

When you think of how little responsibility kids experience in a school situation, it's really no surprise they show so little responsibility in making decisions about life as they grow older. Someone else constantly decides where they will be, when they will be there, and what they will do while there. Kids get very few chances to carry the responsibility ball. Whose fault is it, then, that their first attempts at *stealing* the ball during adolescence often wind up as fumbles?

Compassionate care for an animal is a warm, wonderful path to education, a journey that is truly its own reward. And it won't be long before your child gracefully carries that responsibility for a touchdown.

Simply love a pet.

Simply Listen to the Music

Does music appreciation have to be a forced, forty-five minute, once a week drag? Not if your home stereo offers a banquet of musical treats.

Music affects the environment, wherever it is. With music, a school gymnasium turns into a dance hall, supper transforms into a romantic dinner, a campfire gathering becomes a songfest. Music can positively affect your home environment—and its inhabitants' spirits, too.

Introduce your child's ears to the wide variety of musical expression that fills our world. Your youngsters will like some sounds more than others; find more of those tapes, CDs, or records. (Some of our favorite records cost us twenty-five cents at a yard sale.) Read the cover notes together—interest leads to understanding which leads to knowledge.

Observe the effect of the music on your child. You'll get a sense of what music is conducive to which activities. I'm not talking about the rumors that certain classical selections are conducive to higher test scores, for you won't be administering tests. You'll see that some music creates anxiety or tension. Other music relaxes your child and creates an environment that increases well-being. Any activity she will pursue—whether baking a cake or building a toothpick bridge or bathing the dog or reading an exciting novel— is enriched because of her personal well-being.

Scientists have proven music helps everything from surgery recovery to growing plants. It's just as good for growing children, too. At home you can fill your youngster's life with music. Alternate between Broadway show tunes, a little country, a little jazz, a few Gregorian chants or Rachmaninoff's Symphonic Dances.

Music should be everyone's choice. If you're lucky and serve the music banquet to your child before he gets the idea that any-thing besides grunge or rap tastes bad, you're way ahead of the game. If not, you'll need to decide how much rap you can take. Just keep the faith that tasting enough different sounds will lead to a wider diet. And don't forget that music appreciation can lead to an interest in learning about and playing an instrument.

Most importantly, your child realizes that music is a beautiful, creative expression of life, not a school class one need swallow hard and endure until she can get some rap on her Walkman. Simply crank up the stereo and...listen to the music.

Simply Pursue Your Dreams

Here you are, standing at the threshold of a new way of thinking and living. You're ready to take on the responsibility of your children's education, a responsibility that, up until now, you've considered the private territory of college-trained state employees speaking educationese. You're shaking in your Reeboks.

You have two choices. Give in to your conditioning that everyone needs to be taught, that the institution's way is the only way to learn, and suffer defeat before you even begin. Or you can counteract your conditioning by engaging in activities that help build your confidence and reveal the truth that you are a more capable guide for your children's true education than anyone.

Think of all those things you've been meaning to do if only you had the time—needlework, writing, chair caning, floral design, karate, or perhaps a home business. Learning all you can about your favorite pursuit is the first step to accomplishing it. Then practice, practice, and more practice. Make your mistakes, learn some more, and keep on going. As your ability increases, so does your confidence. Before long you'll start thinking of yourself as a writer or designer or businessperson. So will other people—including your children. Right before their eyes, mom or dad demonstrates the universal life skills that help your children grow into lifelong learners.

The very best teacher has always been and will always be "example." Frank Smith, author of *Insult to Intelligence: The Bureaucratic Invasion of Our Classrooms*, is a leading authority on reading, writing, and children's literacy. Listen to his conclusions on the characteristics of a good teacher:

> Good teachers respond instinctively to the way in which children—and adults—learn, without direction from outside authorities. Good teachers never rely on programs or tests and they resist external control when it is thrust upon them. They do not allow themselves or their "apprentices" to engage in pointless ritualistic activ-

ities. Instead, these teachers manifest attitudes and behavior that learners become interested in manifesting themselves, and then these teachers help learners to manifest such attitudes and behaviors for themselves. Such teachers attract and indenture apprentices without knowing they are doing so... Indeed, they are learners themselves.

You can wait around and hope your child meets a good teacher or two during his twelve-year sentence in public school. Or you can, with courage and trust, develop and display the characteristics of a good teacher 1) in the comfort of your home, 2) pursuing a personally meaningful interest, 3) saving the money you thought you would need to pay someone else to teach you.

You need only become adept at one small, "doable" interest to gather a good dose of confidence. This confidence seeps into other aspects of your life without your awareness, just as an intravenous dose of medicine silently works its way into your bloodstream to restore health. *What* you accomplish is not the point. It's the fact that you set forth on the journey. It's the fact that you do accomplish something. As an old aphorism tells us, education is what remains when the lessons have been forgotten.

What remains for you and your family is confidence, the flowering of the seeds of trust and courage planted in your lives.

Simply pursue your dreams.

CHAPTER SIXTEEN

IMPLICATIONS FOR THE GREATER SOCIETY

I can't help thinking of the Venetian Republic in their last half-century. Like us, they had once been fabulously lucky. They had become rich, as we did, by accident. They had acquired immense political skills, just as we have. A good many of them were tough-minded, realistic, patriotic men. They knew, just as clearly as we know, that the current of history had begun to flow against them. Many of them gave their minds to working out ways to keep going. It would have meant breaking the pattern into which they had crystallised. They were fond of the pattern, just as we are fond of ours. They never found the will to break it.

—C. P. Snow

I t might have been simpler for C.P. to say: Nothing stays the same. Change is inevitable. Those societies that refuse to bend with the winds of change shall perish.

People—individuals—take the first step on that journey to change. Before setting foot on the path to societal improvement, the individuals who fuel that society are obligated to first look at what we've created *as it is*. Not as it used to be. Not as we would like it to be. As it is. And as it is, it's not a pretty sight.

There's a lot that's good in this country. But when it comes to the founding principles of life, liberty, and pursuit of happiness of its individuals, things could be much, much better. Among industrialized nations, America is #1 in military spending ($290 billion), valiantly defending her borders. But what is she today defending? Apparently, her other #1 rankings—in murder and car accidents. And the $425 billion price tag on fourteen million *reported* crimes. Yes, America's people could be much, much happier, not to mention kinder.

There are many who realize that the education current has begun to flow against us. They address conferences, they write volumes, they beg for every scrap of media attention they can garner. Yet the many perils of institutionalized education that these people warn are wounding our very spirits—grades, age-grouping, tracking, programmatic instruction, competition, isolation, early starts, incessant testing—are the same aspects that government-controlled schools *intensify* each time our failures come under scrutiny. What insanity!

The education current has, in fact, been working against us for so long we dare not wait any longer to break "the pattern into which we have crystallized." We, the people who through our collective energy give life to our society, must find the will to break it.

"What we call necessary institutions," wrote Alexis de Tocqueville, "are often no more than institutions to which we have grown accustomed." Shall our conditioned comfort with the familiar stop us from questioning its value?

"A society whose schools are inhumane is not likely to be humane itself," said Charles E. Silberman in *Crisis in the Classroom*. Shall our conditioned inhumanity allow us to forcefully herd our children into an institution that grows more dangerous and violent daily?

Listen carefully to what those with intimate experience within the institution warn:

Retired New York State Teacher of the Year John Taylor Gatto reveals, "The children I teach are uneasy with intimacy or candor. They cannot deal with genuine intimacy because of a lifelong habit of preserving a secret self inside an outer personality made up of artificial bits and pieces of behavior borrowed from television, or acquired to manipulate teachers." Shall our conditioned hypocrisy forever leave our children emotionally crippled?

"By focusing only upon what is observable and quantifiable, [school] accountability obscures and trivializes our view of life by creating a one-dimensional lens," said Thomas S. Popkewitz in *Paradigm and Ideology in Educational Research*. Shall our conditioned blindness let us lead our children off the cliff?

Emeritus Professor of Chemistry Joel H. Hildebrand (University of California Berkeley) laments, "The invention of IQ did a great disservice to creativity in education... Individuality, personality, originality, are too precious to be meddled with by amateur psychiatrists whose patterns for a 'wholesome personality' are inevitably their own." Shall our conditioned mediocrity close the door to genius?

"It's easier," claimed Massachusetts Institute of Technology Professor Jerrold Zacharias, "to put man on the moon than to reform the public schools." Shall the weight of our dead horse break our children's backs?

Perhaps the most basic warning comes from Christopher Hills. His conclusion illustrates that change in our approach to education is imperative if we are to create the type of society we would prefer our children to inherit. Hills cautions that only "when the general body of educated opinion believes that the laws of consciousness are as real as any laws of physics, then there can be nuclear changes in the structure of society." Shall the conditioned unconsciousness our society induces be its very end?

We have been warned—over and over and over again. The call,

to date, has mainly been addressed to those whose perch in lofty political places is far too distant from the daily struggle for meaning and mere survival that our children and communities engage in. It has, for too long, fallen on ears ringing with a cacophony of false education's symptoms, sending those who possess the ability to stop the source of dis-ease running around like self-important little ants. They're preparing to smear our landscape with additional prisons to institutionalize more of those for whom our current schools have done their worst jobs. We need the art of education. They're going to revamp the welfare system. We need the art of education. They're going to flood America's streets with more police. We need the art of education. They're going to tighten their chokehold on the current education system with more of what doesn't work. We need the art of education to grow up healthy and sane in the first place.

Goals 2000, the nation's latest federal education law, just may be the straw that breaks the education institution's back. After all, how tightly must something be grasped before the life drains out of it? Study our education history, folks. You'll notice a steady decline in quality, including the very basic measure of literacy rate, starting with compulsory attendance laws. At the same time, costs increase in relation to—you guessed it—the amount of federal government involvement.

Today, Goals 2000 brings you not one, but three new layers of bureaucracy that are supposed to fix what we, the people, have not. Number one is your previously untried *National Education Goals Panel* whose job it is to "report on progress toward achieving" the *National Education Goals.* Number two will "develop *voluntary* academic standards and assessments." Meet your *National Education Standards and Improvement Council.* And finally, your *National Skill Standards Board* is going to "promote the development and adoption of occupational standards *to ensure that American workers are among the best trained in the world."*

These, my friends, are words from President William Clinton's letter to the Congress of the United States shortly before the bureaucracy thickened with the passage of Goals 2000. It seems trained workers are the goal of at least one of our three new control groups. It seems our children's happiness, our children's fulfillment, our children's *education* are not among the federal controllers' concerns.

Compulsory attendance, or forced herding, is rapidly evolving into compulsory education, or forced acceptance of premeditated, predigested, prescribed thinking, behavior, values, and vocations. How far in the wrong direction are we willing to go on the road to total conditioning? "The cost of removing human error," says Frank Smith, author of *Insult to Intelligence: The Bureaucratic Invasion of Our Classrooms*, "has been the removal of all humanity and the reduction of education to trivia."

In his April 3, 1994 *Los Angeles Times* syndicated column on Goals 2000, Cal Thomas asks, "How should parents respond to this latest government power grab? Just as they would if they knew their children's school was on fire—they should get them out, fast."

The psychological, emotional, and spiritual harm created by public school is as real—and deadly—as fire. *Your* eyes must see what really is. *Your* ears must acknowledge the cry. The truth of schooling's hidden curriculum must penetrate beyond your rational mind into the heart and soul of you. It's time to wake up!

"Schools should be learning emporia, places where people congregate to learn, and no one should be there if they do not want to participate in learning—whether their role is to be a student, a teacher, or an administrator," says Frank White, Harvard Ph.D. These learning emporia are the learning centers explored in "It Takes a Village to Raise a Child." They can be our children's saving grace. And they can only exist when and where we, the people, reclaim our children, our communities, and our Selves.

How? We simply say "no thank you" when others offer to herd our kids off to be conditioned with the same values, interests, and skills that have made our society what it is today. The moment we say no thank you, we assume responsibility. *We* create the freedom necessary to replace false values, interests, and skills with real, meaningful, useful ones that bring out the best within each of us. And that which is within is far richer, more beautiful, and more important than the "sameness" we spend so much time and money trying to create.

The implications for society are dramatic, frighteningly so, if we remain asleep, more comfortable with the thought of things as they are than with the uncertainty that accompanies the unknown. At the same time, the implications for society are exciting if we wake up, decide there is something better for our families, and create it, using as our only tools the trust we place in our Selves, the courage to change what we can, and the truth inherent in a natural path.

As you may have guessed, I prefer the excitement of creating something new, not because I've always been a reckless adventurer (I haven't), but because family centered education as "something better" has benefits daily displayed under my own roof and within my community. I wouldn't have believed it—yet I'm experiencing it.

Our education crisis is a crisis with a depth and magnitude sending tremors throughout every stratum of society. This crisis transcends the economic, ethnic, religious, and political walls within which anyone may mistakenly think he will find refuge.

Whether we accept it or not, whether we *like* it or not, nature is stepping in—the volcano is erupting. We can stand still and suffer a painfully slow demise under the lava flow. Or we can get out of our own way and climb the newly created mountain to enjoy a whole new view.

But first, we must stop fueling the crisis with our children.

> The young, with their keen noses for hypocrisy, are in fact adept readers—but not of books. They are society-smart rather than school-smart, and what they read so acutely are the social signals emanating from the world in which they will have to make a living.
>
> —Benjamin R. Barber, "*America Skips School*," *Harpers*, November, 1993

If our present social signals, so well read by our children, confuse and anger and destroy their spirit, they are shamefully wrong. The art of education, accessible to many and practiced at home, offers families the unique ability and means to change those signals. Indeed, we can throw overboard the current definitions of success, livelihood, learning, school, genius and family that drive us, en masse, to seek various forms of professional help. We can start anew, redefining for ourselves and our families the purpose and meaning of the lives we lead.

It starts with you. In a speech called *Choices and Change*, former First Lady Barbara Bush told Wellesley College's 1990 graduating class, "Your success as a family, our success as a society, depends *not* on what happens at the White House, but on what happens inside your house." Only you can determine what's happening inside your home. Only you can change what's happening inside your home. Only you can reclaim your children, your community, and your Self.

In his June 6, 1994 address at the 50th anniversary of D-Day in France, President William Clinton declared, "Freedom's purpose is progress." I wholeheartedly disagree. Freedom has no innate purpose. Rather, it is a condition, a necessary base state of being vital to the natural expansion of human consciousness inherent in true education. Education's value hinges on the freedom that surrounds it. Freedom—of body, mind, and spirit—is the only setting in which life may move, unencumbered, toward happiness.

And if you are concerned about the end of the education institution as we know it, fear not. The vast majority of family centered educators ask for and take nothing from the institution. They are not usurping energy from what exists, for that energy flows in so many false directions it is dissipated beyond human benefit.

What appears to be unfolding is nothing less than the creation of energy where none existed before. Homeschoolers are discovering and bringing forth their own energy, their unique creative intelligence. They have summoned forth the necessary courage and trust, and empower themselves, their children, and their communities.

Today, family centered education is still only a mere whisper of a promise that life for you, your children, and your community can be happier, healthier, and more meaningful. That whisper does not yet rise above the roar of social discord. But don't worry. As Jesuit paleontologist Pierre Teilhard de Chardin observed, "A truth once seen, even by a single mind, always ends by imposing itself on the totality of human consciousness." Don't worry.

We, the people, are teaching ourselves.

APPENDIXES

No endeavor that is worthwhile is simple in prospect; if it is right, it will be simple in retrospect.
—Edward Teller

APPENDIX A - HOMESCHOOL "ALUMNI"

John Quincy Adams	U.S. President
Konrad Adenauer	Statesman
Hans Christian Anderson	Favored children's author
Alexander Graham Bell	Inventor
Pearl Buck	Pulitzer and Nobel prize winning author, humanitarian
William F. Buckley, Jr.	Author, columnist, TV personality, and vocabulary wizard
John Burroughs	Naturalist, author
Andrew Carnegie	Industrialist
George Washington Carver	Scientist
Charles Chaplin	Actor
Winston Churchill	Prime Minister of England
Agatha Christie	Author
George Rogers Clark	Explorer
Noel Coward	Playwright
Pierre Curie	Scientist
Charles Dickens	Author
Thomas Edison	Inventor
Benjamin Franklin	Statesman, inventor, author
William Henry Harrison	U. S. President
Bret Harte	Author
Patrick Henry	Statesman, author
Stonewall Jackson	Confederate General
Robert E. Lee	Confederate General
C. S. Lewis	Author
Abraham Lincoln	U. S. President
Douglas MacArthur	U. S. Army General
Cyrus McCormick	Inventor
Tamara McKinney	1983-84 World Cup skier
James Madison	U. S. President
Claude Monet	Artist, painter
George Patton	U. S. Army General
William Penn	Statesman, author, human liberty advocate
Franklin Delano Roosevelt	U. S. President
Albert Schweitzer	Physician, humanitarian
George Bernard Shaw	Author
Frank Vandiver	Texas A & M University President
Leonardo da Vinci	Artist, inventor
George Washington	U. S. President
Woodrow Wilson	U. S. President
Wright Brothers	Inventors
Andrew Wyeth	Artist, painter
Jamie Wyeth	Artist, painter

APPENDIX B - NOTES

MEET YOUR MAKERS

1. Carroll Quigley, *Tragedy and Hope: A History of the World in Our Time*, New York, The MacMillan Company, 1966, p. 62.
2. Ibid., p. 53.
3. John Gatto, "Absolute Absolution," *Skole - The Journal of Alternative Education*, Winter, 1994, Volume XI, No. 1, p. 26.
4. Stephanie Coontz, *The Way We Never Were*, New York, Basic Books, 1992, p. 134.
5. Richard Duesenberg, "Economic Liberties and the Law," *Imprimis*, April, 1994, p. 1.
6. Ivan Illich, *Deschooling Society*, New York, Harper & Row, Publishers, 1971, p. 47.
7. *Ibid.*, p. 39.
8. *Ibid.*, p. 39.
9. Gatto, *op. cit.*, p. 28.
10. Merrill D. Peterson, *The Jefferson Image in the American Mind*, New York, Oxford University Press, 1962, pp. 239-240.
11. From Rothbard, *Education, Free and Compulsory*, p. 42.

IS THAT ALL THERE IS?

1. Benjamin R. Barber, "America Skips School," *Harper's*, November, 1993, p. 42.
2. Ibid
3. Ibid
4. Allan Bloom, *The Closing of the American Mind*, New York, Simon & Schuster, 1987, p. 38.
5. *Ibid.*, book jacket.
6. Maharishi Mahesh Yogi, *Science of Being and Art of Living*, New York, Signet, 1968, p. 210.

THE EDUCATION PYRAMID

1. G. I. Gurdjieff, *Herald of the Coming Good*, Paris, no publisher given; reprinted, New York, Weiser, 1970, p. 30.
2. Jane M. Healy, Ph.D., *Endangered Minds: Why Children Don't Think and What We Can Do About It*, Touchstone, New York, Simon and Schuster, Inc., 1990, p.151.
3. Ibid., p. 81.
4. Christopher Hills, *Nuclear Evolution*, Boulder Creek, CA, University of the Trees Press, 1977, p. 504.

5. Gary Zukav, *The Dancing Wu Li Masters: An Overview of the New Physics*, New York, William Morrow and Co., Inc., 1979, p. 115.

6. Henry Stapp, "S-Matrix Interpretation of Quantum Theory," *Physical Review*, D3, 1971, 1303.

ADDICTED TO EXPERTS

1. Alfie Kohn, *Punished By Rewards: The Trouble with Gold Stars, Incentive Plans, A's, Praise, and Other Bribes*, New York, Houghton Mifflin Co., 1993, p.150.

2. Ivan Illich, *Deschooling Society*, New York, Harper & Row, Publishers, 1971, p. 47.

3. *Ibid.*, p. 39.

AS YOU SOW SO SHALL YOU REAP

1. Benjamin R. Barber, "America Skips School," *Harper's*, November, 1993, p. 39.

2. CBS Evening News, March 28, 1994.

3. William E. Brock, U. S. Secretary of Labor, to Senate Committee on Labor and Human Resources, *New York Times*, January 14, 1987.

4. Benjamin R. Barber, "America Skips School," *Harper's*, November, 1993, p. 41.

5. John Taylor Gatto, "A Different Kind of Teacher," Educare reprint, 14600 N. E. 28th St., Vancouver, WA 98682, p. 10.

EXAMINING PRIORITIES

1. Jane M. Healy, Ph.D., *Endangered Minds: Why Children Don't Think and What We Can Do About It*, Touchstone, New York, Simon and Schuster, Inc., p. 91.

2. Christopher Lasch, *Haven in a Heartless World: The Family Besieged*, New York, Basic Books, 1977, p. xvi.

3. John Skurnowicz, "It's Time Parents Take Back Their Children," *Oakland Press*, Pontiac, MI, December, 1993, pg. unknown (Skurnowicz, retired from IBM, is a Michigan certified teacher).

4. Linda Dobson, "News Watch," *Home Education Magazine*, March/April, 1994, p. 48.

5. *Newsweek*, February 7, 1994, p. 15.

6. Nicholas Lemann, "Naperville: Stressed Out in Suburbia," *Harper's*, November, 1989, pp. 34-48.

7. *American Heritage Dictionary of the English Language*, New York, American Heritage Publishing Co., Inc., 1973.

8. Bruce J. Christensen, "On the Streets: Homeless in America," *The Family in America*, June, 1990, p. 7.

9. Benjamin R. Barber, "America Skips School," *Harper's*, November, 1993, p. 43.

10. Mitchell, Wister, and Burch, "The Family Environment: Leaving the Parental Home," *Journal of Marriage and the Family*, 51(1989), pp. 605-613.
11. "Marital Stability Throughout the Child Rearing Years," *Demography*, 27(1990), pp. 55-63.
12. Stephanie Coontz, *The Way We Never Were*, New York, Basic Books, 1992, p. 285.

CREATING YOUR FAMILY'S PERSONAL EDUCATION PHILOSOPHY

1. Marilyn Ferguson, *The Aquarian Conspiracy*, Los Angeles, CA, St. Martin's Press, 1980, p. 282.
2. Paul Dressel, "Facts and Fancy in Assigning Grades," *Basic College Quarterly*, 2(1957), pp. 6-12.

EXPLODING THE TOP FIVE MYTHS ABOUT FAMILY CENTERED EDUCATION

1. Name of a national "unschooling" periodical, *Growing Without Schooling*, Holt Associates, Inc., 2269 Massachusetts Ave., Cambridge, MA 02140.
2. Jane M. Healy, Ph.D., *Endangered Minds: Why Children Don't Think and What We Can Do About It*, Touchstone, New York, Simon and Schuster, Inc., 1990, pp. 71-72.
3. Taylor, J.W. (1986) *Self-concept in home-schooling children*. Doctoral dissertation. Andrews University. Berrien Springs, MI.
   Shyers, L.E. (1992). *A comparison of social adjustment between home-schooled and traditionally schooled students*. Doctoral dissertation. Univ. of Florida. Miami.
4. Larry and Susan Kaseman, "The Politics of Education," from *Alternatives in Education*, Tonasket, WA, Home Education Press, 1992, p. 55.
5. Linda Dobson, "The Trouble with Socialization," *Home Education Magazine*, September, 1987, pp. 10-11.

COPING WITH BEING A PIONEER ON THE ROAD TO FREEDOM

1. Alexis de Tocqueville, *Democracy In America*, Vol. II, Pt. 2, Ch. 1.
2. "Socialization of Homeschoolers Studied by University of Michigan," University of Michigan press release reviewed in *At Home in New England*, Number 23, p. 1.
3. Brenda Hunter, Ph.D., *Home By Choice: Facing the Effects of Mother's Absence*, Portland, OR, Multnomah Press, 1991, p. 77.
4. "Homeschool Court Report," reported in *LUNO (Learning Unlimited Network of Oregon)*, 9:3, April 4, 1994, p. 10.
5. Peter Brimelow and Leslie Spencer, "The National Extortion Association?" *Forbes*, June 7, 1993, pp. 72-84. (Beg, borrow, or steal this coverage of the

National Education Association. Then read the special section of readers' responses in a subsequent issue, and make up your own mind. But read it.)

I AM THE CAPTAIN OF MY SOUL

1. Debbie Goldberg, "There's No School Like Home," *Washington Post Education Review,* April 3, 1994, pp. 4-5.
2. Thomas McArdle, "Do Kids Learn More at Home?" *Investor's Business Daily,* March 14, 1994, p. 1.
3. Isabel Lyman, M.A., "Martin Luther King III Encourages Homeschoolers," *Moore Report International,* January/February, 1994, p. 5.

IT TAKES A VILLAGE TO RAISE A CHILD

1. Cal Thomas, "Children Don't Need These 'Goals,'", *Cincinnati Enquirer,* April 3, 1994.
2. Craig Lancto, "No More Pencils, No More Books, No More Teacher's Dirty Looks," *Fairfax (VA) Journal,* May 9, 1994.
3. Gene Lehman, "Schooling or Learning," *Learning Unlimited Network of Oregon,* November 26, 1990, p. 4.
4. Frank Smith, *Insult to Intelligence: The Bureaucratic Invasion of Our Classrooms,* New York, Arbor House, 1986, p. 59.
5. John Taylor Gatto, "Confederacy of Dunces: The Tyranny of Compulsory Schooling," *The Sun,* Issue 204, December, 1992, pp. 4-12.
6. Jerry Mintz, "Homeschool Support Groups and Resource Centers," *Home Education Magazine,* September/October, 1991, pp. 33-35.
7. Janie B. Cheaney, "A Cooperative Home School Learning Center," *Home Education Magazine,* January/February, 1991, pp. 13-14, 50.
8. "Dropout Rates in the United States: 1992," U. S. Department of Education Office of Educational Research and Improvement (NCES 93-464), p. vi.
9. Roderick F. McPhee, "School Reform: Much Ado About Nothing," *Vital Speeches,* September 15, 1992, p. 733.
10. Raymond S. Moore and Dorothy Moore, "When Education Becomes Abuse: A Different Look at the Mental Health of Children," *Journal of School Health,* Volume 56, Number 2, February, 1986, pp. 73-74.
11. H. G. McCurdy, "The Childhood Pattern of Genius," *Horizon,* 1960, 2:33-38.

APPENDIX—C LEARN MORE ABOUT IT

CHOOSING YOUR OWN FAMILY'S EDUCATION
(SEE ALSO: ON-LINE RESOURCES)

ANOTHER PERSPECTIVE ON EDUCATION

Armstrong, Thomas, *The Myth of the A.D.D. Child* (Putnam, NY 1996)
  Awakening Your Child's Natural Genius: Enhancing Curiosity, Creativity and Learning Ability (Los Angeles, Jeremy Tarcher, 1991)
  In Their Own Way: Discovering and Encouraging Your Child's Personal Learning Style (Los Angeles, Jeremy Tarcher, Inc., 1987)

Baldwin, Rahima, *You Are Your Child's First Teacher* (Berkeley, CA, Celestial Arts, 1989)

Dyer, Dr. Wayne W., *What Do You Really Want for Your Children?* (New York, William Morris and Co., Inc., 1985)

Gardner, Howard, *Frames of Mind* (New York, Basic Books, 1985)

Goelitz, Jeffrey, *The Ultimate Kid: Levels of Learning that Make a Difference* (Boulder Creek, CA, University of the Trees Press, 1986)

Gurdjieff, G. I., *Meetings with Remarkable Men* (New York, Dutton, 1968)

Healy, Jane M., *Endangered Minds: Why Children Don't Think and What We Can Do About It* (New York, Simon and Schuster, 1990)

Hendricks, Gay and Wills, Russell, *The Centering Book* (Englewood Cliffs, N.J., Prentice Hall, 1985)

Herzog, Stephanie, *Joy in the Classroom* (Boulder Creek, CA, University of the Trees Press, 1982)

Kline, Peter, *The Everyday Genius: Restoring Children's Natural Joy of Learning* (Arlington, VA, Great Ocean Publishers, 1988)

Kiyosaki, Robert T., *If You Want to Be Rich and Happy, Don't Go to School* (Lower Lake, CA, Aslan Publishing, 1993)

Krishnamurti, *Education and the Significance of Life* (NY, Harper & Row, 1953)

Leue, Mary, editor, *Challenging the Giant: The Best of Skole, The Journal of Alternative Education* (Albany, NY, Down-to-Earth Books, 1992)

Luvmour, Josette and Sambhava, *Natural Learning Rhythms: How and When Children Learn* (Berkeley, CA, Celestial Arts, 1993)

Steiner, Rudolf, *The Four Temperments* (New York, Anthroposophic Press, 1971)

COMPETITION, TESTS, TRACKING, LABELS, GRADES, ETC.

Bloom, Allan, *The Closing of the American Mind* (NY, Simon & Schuster, 1987)

Coles, Gerald, *The Learning Mystique: A Critical Look at "Learning Disabilities"* (New York, Ballantine, 1989)

Elkind, David, *The Hurried Child* (Reading, MA, Addison-Wesley, 1981)

Fair Test, *Standardized Tests and Our Children: A Guide to Testing Reform* (Cambridge, MA, National Center for Fair and Open Testing, 1990)

Gould, Stephen Jay, *The Mismeasure of Man* (New York, W. W. Norton, 1981)

Granger, Bill and Lori, *The Magic Feather: The Truth About Special Education* (New York, E.P. Dutton, 1986)

Illich, Ivan, *Deschooling Society* (New York, Harper & Row, Publishers, 1971)

Kohn, Alfie, *Punished By Rewards: The Trouble with Gold Stars, Incentive Plans, A's, Praise, and Other Bribes* (New York, Houghton Mifflin, 1993)

No Contest: The Case Against Competition (NY, Houghton Mifflin, 1992)

Kozol, Jonathan, *Illiterate America* (New York, Anchor Press/Doubleday, 1985)

McGuinness, Diane, *When Children Don't Learn* (New York, Basic Books, 1985)

Oakes, Jeannie, *Keeping Track: How Schools Structure Inequality* (New Haven, CT, Yale University Press, 1985)

Owen, David, *None of the Above: Behind the Myth of Scholastic Aptitude* (Boston, Houghton Mifflin Co., 1981)

Sheffer, Susannah, *Everyone is Able: Exploding the Myth of Learning Disabilities* (Cambridge, MA, Holt Associates, 1987)

Silberman, Charles E., *Crisis in the Classroom* (New York, Random House, 1970)

Smith, Frank, *Insult to Intelligence: The Bureaucratic Invasion of Our Classrooms* (New York, Arbor House, 1986)

Sowell, Thomas, *Inside American Education: The Decline, The Deception, The Dogmas* (New York, The Free Press/Macmillan, Inc., 1993)

Strenio, Andrew J., Jr., *The Testing Trap* (New York, Rawson, Wade Publishing, Inc., 1981)

EDUCATION HISTORY

Arons, Stephen, *Compelling Belief: The Culture of American Schooling* (New York, New Press/McGraw-Hill Book Co., 1983)

Gatto, John, *Dumbing Us Down: The Hidden Curriculum of Compulsory Schooling* (Philadelphia, New Society Publishers, 1991)

Leonard, George B., *Education and Ecstasy* (New York, Delacorte Press, 1968)

Miller, Ron, *What Are Schools For? Holistic Education in American Culture,* (Brandon, VT, Holistic Education Press, 1990)

FAMILY CENTERED EDUCATION

Cohen, Cafi, *And What About College? How Homeschooling Leads to Admissions to the Best Colleges and Universitites* (Cambridge, MA, Holt Associates 1997)

Colfax, David and Micki, *Homeschooling for Excellence: How to Take Charge of Your Child's Education—And Why You Absolutely Must* (New York, Warner Books, 1988)

Farenga, Patrick, *The Beginners Guide To Homeschooling* (Cambridge, MA, Holt Associates, 1995)

Gelner, Judy, *College Admissions: A Guide for Homeschoolers* (Sedalia, CO, Poppyseed Press, 1988)

Griffith, Mary, *The Homeschool Handbook* (Rocklin, CA, Prima Publishing, 1997)

Guterson, David, *Family Matters: Why Homeschooling Makes Sense* (Orlando, FL, Harcourt, Brace, Jovanovich, 1992)

Hegener, Mark & Helen, *The Homeschool Reader: Perspectives on Homeschooling* (Tonasket, WA, Home Education Press, 1988/95)

Holt, John, *Learning All the Time: How Small Children Begin to Read, Write, Count, and Investigate the World, Without Being Taught* (New York, Addison-Wesley Publishing Co., 1989)

Teach Your Own (London, Lighthouse Books, 1997)

The Homeschool Exchange, POB 1378, Boerne, TX 78006

Kaseman, Larry, Susan, *Taking Charge Through Homeschooling: Personal and Political Empowerment* (Stoughton, WI, Koshkonong Press, 1990)

Llewellyn, Grace, *The Teenage Liberation Handbook : How to Quit School and Get a Real Life and Education* (Eugene, OR, Lowry House, 1991)

Leistico, Agnes, *I Learn Better by Teaching Myself* and *Still Teaching Ourselves* (Cambridge, MA, Holt Associates, 1997))

Moore, Ray, Dorothy, *The Successful Homeschooling Family Handbook: A Creative and Stress-Free Approach to Homeschooling* (Nashville, TN, Thomas Nelson Publishers, 1994)

Home Grown Kids: A Practical Handbook for Teaching Your Children at Home (Waco, TX, Word Books, 1981)

School Can Wait (Washougal, WA, Hewett Research Foundation, 1982)

Reed, Donn, *The Home School Source Book* (Lyndon, VT, Brook Farm Books, 1991)

Rupp, Rebecca, *Good Stuff: Learning Tools for All Ages* (Cambridge, MA, Holt Associates, 1997)

Sheffer, Susannah, *A Sense of Self: Listening To Homeschooled Adolescent Girls* (Portsmouth, NH, Heinemann, 1995)

ORGANIZATIONS TO CONTACT FOR MORE
INFORMATION ON EDUCATION ALTERNATIVES

Alliance for Parental Involvement in Education, P. O. Box 59, East Chatham, NY 12060-0059; 518-392-6900

Alternative Education Resource Organization, 417 Roslyn Rd., Roslyn Heights, NY   11577; 516-621-2195

Canadian Alliance of Home Educators, 272 Hwy #5, RR 1, St. George, Ontario N0E1N0; 519-448-4001

The Catholic Home Educator, POB 420225, San Diego, CA 92142

Drinking Gourd, The, P. O. Box 2557, Redmond, WA 98073; 206-836-0336

The Eclectic Homeschool, POB 736, Bellevue, NE 68005-0736

Holt Associates / *Growing Without Schooling*, 2269 Massachusetts Ave., Cambridge, MA   02140; 617-864-3100

Home Education Magazine, P. O. Box 1083, Tonasket, WA 98855; 509-486-1351

Homeschooling Information Clearinghouse, P.O. Box 293023, Sacramento, CA 95829-3023; 916-422-2879

Moore Foundation, Box 1, Camas, WA   98607; 206-835-5500

National Center For Fair And Open Testing (Fair Test), P. O. Box 1272, Harvard Square Station, Cambridge, MA   02238; 617-864-4810

National Homeschool Association, P. O. Box 290, Hartland, MI 48353-0290 (513) 772-9580

CHOOSING A DIFFERENT WAY TO PARENT AND PLAY
ANOTHER PERSPECTIVE ON PARENTING AND PLAY

Berends, Polly Berrien, *Whole Child/Whole Parent: A Spiritual and Practical Guide to Parenthood* (New York, Harper and Row, 1983)

Chinmoy, Sri, *A Child's Heart and A Child's Dreams* (New York, Aum Publications, 1986)

Cornell, Joseph, *Sharing Nature with Children: The Classic Parents' and Teachers' Nature Awareness Guidebook* (Nevada City, CA, Ananda Publications, 1979)

Deacove, Jim, *Games Manual of Non-Competitive Games* (Ontario, Canada, Family Pastimes, 1974)

Jenkins, Peggy, *The Joyful Child: A Sourcebook of Activities and Ideas for Releasing Children's Natural Joy* (Tucson, AZ, Harbinger House, Inc., 1989)

Pearce, Joseph Chilton, *Magical Child* (New York, Dutton, 1974)

Rozman, Deborah, *Meditation for Children: Pathways to Happiness, Harmony, Creativity and Fun for the Family* (Lower Lake, California, Aslan Publishing, 1989)

Meditating with Children: The Art of Concentration and Centering (Boulder Creek, CA, University of the Trees Press, 1988)

Sobel, Jeffrey, *Everybody Wins* (New York, Walker Publications, 1984)

CHOOSING YOUR OWN LIFESTYLE:
BOOKS FOR LIFESTYLE ALTERNATIVES

Berkowitz, Bill, *Community Dreams: Ideas for Enriching Neighborhood and Community Life* (San Luis Obispo, CA, Impact Publishers, 1984)

Dominguez, Joe and Vicki Robin, *Your Money or Your Life: Transforming Your Relationship with Money and Achieving Financial Independence* (New York, Viking, 1992)

Johnson, Warren, *Muddling Toward Frugality* (San Fancisco, Sierra Club, 1978)

Nearing, Helen, *Our Home Made of Stone* (Camden, ME, Down East Books, 1983)

Simple Food for the Good Life (New York, Delta/Eleanor Friede, 1980)

Saltzman, Amy, *Downshifting: Reinventing Success on a Slower Track* (New York, HarperCollins, 1991)

NEWSLETTERS TO HELP YOU LIVE ON LESS

Cheapskate Monthly, P. O. Box 2135, Paramount, CA   90723

Frugal Times, 12534 Valley View Street #234, Garden Grove, CA   92645

Live Better for Less, 21 E. Chestnut St., Chicago, IL   60611

Living Cheap News, P. O. Box 700058, San Jose, CA   95170

On a Shoestring, P. O. Box 2025, Livingston, NJ   07039

The Penny Pincher, P. O. Box 809, Kings Park, NY   11754

Pinch-A-Penny, P. O. Box 91214, Chattanooga, TN   37412

Skinflint News, 1460 Noell Boulevard, Palm Harbor, FL   34683

The Smart Skinflint, P. O. Box 62822, Virginia Beach, VA   23466

Thrifty Living, P. O. Box 416, South Wellfleet, MA   02663

The Tightwad Gazette, RR 1, Box 3570, Leeds, ME   04263

PHILOSOPHY OF ALTERNATIVE LIFESTYLES

Cloninger, Claire, *A Place Called Simplicity: The Quiet Beauty of Simple Living* (Eugene, OR. Harvest House, 1993)

Daly, Herman E., *For the Common Good* (Boston, Beacon Press, 1989)

Elgin, Duane, *Voluntary Simplicity* (New York, William Morrow, 1981)

Nearing, Helen, *Loving and Leaving the Good Life* (Post Mills, VT, Chelsea Green Publishing Co., 1992)

Nearing, Scott and Helen, *Living the Good Life* (New York, Schocken, 1954)

Nearing, Scott, *Freedom: Promise and Menace* (Harborside, ME, Social Science Institute, 1961)

The Making of a Radical (New York, Harper/Colophon, 1972)

Shi, David, *The Simple Life* (New York, Oxford University Press, 1985)

VandenBroeck, Goldian, *Less is More: The Art of Voluntary Poverty* (Rochester, Inner Traditions International, 1991)

Wachtel, Paul, *The Poverty of Affluence* (Philadelphia, PA, New Society Publishers, 1989)

PRACTICAL GUIDES TO LIFESTYLE ALTERNATIVES

At-Home Dads Newsletter, 61 Brightwood Ave., North Andover, MA 01845

Back Home Magazine, P.O. Box 370, Hendersonville, NC 28793; 704-696-3838

Backwoods Home Magazine, 1257 Siskiyou Blvd. #213, Ashland, OR 97520

Country Journal, P.O. Box 8200, Harrisburg, PA 17105

Countryside & Small Stock Journal, W11564B Hwy 64, Withee, WI 54498

Harrowsmith Country Life, P.O. Box 54431, Boulder, CO 80323-4431

Home Power Magazine, P.O. Box 275, Ashland, OR 97520; 916-475-0830

Journal of Family Life, 72 Phillip St., Albany, NY 12202; (518) 432-1578

Mothering Magazine, P.O. Box 1650, Santa Fe, NM 87504; 505-984-8116

Natural Life Magazine, RR 1, St. George, Ontario N0E 1NO Canada

Organic Gardening, P.O. Box 7320, Red Oak, IA 51591; 800-666-2206

Small Farm Advocate, P.O. Box 405, Walthill, NJ 68067; 402-846-5428

Welcome Home Magazine, 5001 W. Broad St. #316, Richmond, VA 23230

TELEVISION

Lappé, Frances Moore, *What to Do After You Turn Off the TV* (New York, Ballantine, 1985)

Mander, Jerry, *Four Arguments for the Elimination of Television* (New York, Morrow Quill, 1978)

Winn, Marie, *The Plug-In Drug: Television, Children and the Family* (New York, Penguin, 1985)

VOLUNTEERISM

Carroll, Andrew, *Volunteer USA* (New York, Fawcett Columbine, 1991)

Dass, Ram and Paul Gorman, *How Can I Help?* (NY, Alfred A. Knopf, 1985)

McMillan, Bill, *Volunteer Vacations* (Chicago, Review Press, 1989)

Wilson, Marlene, *You Can Make a Difference* (Boulder, CO., Volunteer Management Associates, 1990)

ON-LINE RESOURCES

American Homeschool Association On-line Newsletter—subscribe via

AHAonline@aol.com
Family Learning Exchange Online—subscribe via FmlyLrngEx@aol.com
Home Education Magazine On-line Newsletter—subscribe via
HEMnewsltr@aol.com
Home Education Watch—subscribe via HEWatch@aol.com
Lynn's Picks—Top 10 Homeschooling Places to Visit on the Internet -
subscription information via putco@aol.com

Web Sites

Alliance for Parental Involvement in Education
http://www.croton.com/allpie/

Alternative Education Resource Organization
http://www.speakeasy.org/~aero/

Canadian Homeschool Conferences
http://www.flora.org/homeschol-ca/conf/conf.htm

CHN Online Resources
http://www.comenius.org/resource.htm

Cours Cannois International, Ltd.
http://members.aol.com/CraigLanct/index.html

Education Source, The
http://www.edusource.com

Growing Without Schooling Magazine
http://www.holtgws.com

Home Education Magazine
http://www.home-ed-press.com

Home Educator's Family Times
http://outrig.com/hsn/

Home Learning Software
http://members.aol.com/homelearn

Homefires: The Journal of Homeschooling
http://www.homefires.com/

Homeschool Trading Post
http://www.castlegate.net/swapshop/tradpost.htm#sublinks

Homeschooling and the Internet
http://member.aol.com/putco/LColeman.htm

Homeschooling Resources
http://www.eskimo.com/~billb/home.html

Independent Institute
http://www.independent.org/libertytree/

Jon's Homeschool Resource Page
http://www.midnightbeach.com/hs/

Listing of Homeschool Conferences—(not much at press time but promising!)
http://www.sound.net:80/~ejcol/confer.html

Natural Child
http://www.naturalchild.com

Natural Life
www.netroute.net/altpress

Separation of School and State Alliance
www.sepschool.org

INDEX

For additional copies of *The Art of Education* send $18.95 per book plus $4.50 UPS for first copy, .75 per each additional copy to:

Holt Associates/Growing Without Schooling
2269 Massachusetts Ave.
Cambridge, MA 02104
(617) 864-3100

You can request our FREE catalog from the above address.